SIX
PROTOCOLS
OF IT
TRANS
FORMA
TION

Managing the
Transformation of
IT Ecosystems
with Value-Based IT

PATRICK LESANDRINI

Acknowledgements

As a first time author, without a publishing company, I have been fortunate enough to be surrounded by professionals who have helped me move from an idea to delivery. Each of these contributors has played an important role on this journey, and this book would not have been possible without each of their unique talents and contributions:

Rebecca Huehls, Development and Copy Editor, Comet Dog Studio

Adam C Young, Business Strategy & Marketing, Advisory Services Consultant at Grant Thornton, LLP

Kathleen Cunningham, Book and Web Design, Strategic Brand Designer at Kathleen Cunningham Design

I wish to acknowledge the authors who graciously let me reference their publications; their works and names are noted in the bibliography. Also my family, including my wife Natasha, my son Patrick, and my brothers (Kent, Danny & Jay), who endured countless attempts at a first draft with grace and support; thank you for your patience.

I am indebted to my colleagues in the industry, whose feedback and input helped shape my IT transformation philosophy. Additionally, to those colleagues, managers and leaders whose actions and behaviors served as the impetus for writing this book, I thank you for the inspiration.

Finally, I want to thank Merideth Mehlberg for her coaching and mentoring throughout this process. I am not the same person I was when I walked into her office for the first time. The journey of writing this book has forever changed me in ways I will always be grateful for and Merideth was both an inspiration and friend throughout this adventure.

CONTENTS

INTRODUCTION

This book examines the trends that, over the past two decades, promised to help companies reduce costs and improve outcomes for IT organizations but did not succeed. These IT projects and transformations failed — and continue to fail — because they approach IT using only profit-based strategies. Moreover, these profit-based strategies are responsible for unforeseen and unintended consequences in IT organizations, including reduced productivity, lower service levels, cost overruns, and the lack of adoption of new processes and technology.

The IT transformation strategies I examine are popularly known as "cheaper, faster, better" and involve industry best practices, such as ITIL, ITSM, and outsourcing, as well as IT transformation consulting services.

This book is about the things employees talk about when no one is around. It's an affirmation for those who are still living with the consequences of these IT transformations and a wakeup call for those who are responsible for implementing the changes only through the lens of profit. This book is the insider's guide to how companies really think and work.

Most importantly, this book outlines how a company can change IT strategy to drive better outcomes for IT initiatives and services that improve the client's condition while still managing the company's balance sheet.

In Part I, I explore the belief systems, behaviors, and strategies that have shaped the current landscape of IT organizations. After examining how and why these trends have failed companies and their employees, I introduce value-based IT, which offers the scaffolding to provide higher focus on how to manage costs alongside IT's value to the business and lay a more solid foundation for the success of large-scale IT projects and transformations.

Part II explores in-depth how companies can implement this approach, and Part III explains how to sustain the goals and value of IT-transformation through the principles of organizational health.

Taking Stock of IT Project Failure Rates

A 2013 analysis of IT project failure rates estimated that roughly 40 percent of projects costing more than $5 million failed. When research is aggregated for projects below and above this threshold, failure rates are closer to 50 percent. The results of these studies are symptomatic of serious problems across a broad cross-section of industries. Although fully assessing the breadth of this problem is forensically impossible, here are examples of results published over the last 5 years:

- In a 2012 joint study between McKinsey & Company and University of Oxford, researchers found that
  - 17 percent of large IT projects go so badly that they can threaten the company's existence.
  - On average, large IT projects exceed budgets by 45 percent and time estimates by 7 percent but only deliver 44 percent of their predicted value.
- According to an IBM study, only 40 percent of projects have accurate schedules and budgets and deliver their expected quality.
- The Standish Group found that over 80 percent of IT projects cost twice as much as predicted or are never completed.
- Panorama Consulting Solutions conducted a survey of ERP implementations and found that
  - 93 percent took longer than planned.
  - 65 percent were over budget.
  - 79 percent realized less than half the planned benefits.
- In 2011, Geneca, a custom software developer, published a study of software projects and found the following:
  - Unclear business objectives, out-of-sync stakeholders, and excessive rework left 75 percent of project participants lacking confidence that their projects will succeed.
  - 78 percent of respondents reported that the "business is usually or always out of sync with project requirements."

In a 2013 paper, Gartner proposed that project and portfolio management (PPM) leaders should adopt a fail-forward-fast strategy that accepts project failure rates of 20-28 percent as the norm. In other words, companies should assume that nearly a third of all projects will fail. However, I don't believe lowering the bar for expectations is the right answer, especially when value-based IT offers a better solution.

Tracking Outsourcing Failure Rates

As part of "cheaper, faster, better" IT transformations, companies turned to outsourcing as a way to increase scale and quality but drive down costs. Unfortunately, the statistics do not look much better than those for IT project failure rates.

In 2014, IT outsourcing deals show a failure rate well above 50 percent. Organizations with failed outsourcing programs then face the perils of *backsourcing,* the painful process of terminating outsourcing contracts while initiating the process of re-establishing IT operations in-house. When a company backsources, it pays not only the direct costs of operational disruption and penalty fees, but also the indirect costs of transition, which include damage to the company's reputation and damage to relationships with customers, employees, investors, and corporate partners.

For over a decade, companies have been moving IT operations back in-house, and the list of companies doing so is long:

- American Airlines brought back its IT infrastructure from IBM in 2007.
- JPMorgan Chase & Co. terminated a $5 billion contract with IBM in 2002.
- Sainsbury's terminated an outsourcing contract with Accenture after five years.
- McDermott International, Inc., dropped a 10-year global IT outsourcing deal with AT&T's professional services and took back responsibility for design, implementation, and management of its IT services.
- In 2013, Santander, General Motors, and Maybank Singapore announced that they are bringing back offshored work to onshore.

Given the trend in backsourcing, outsourcing IT services looks increasingly like a shortsighted fix rather than a long-term solution. Indeed, the very same companies that touted the outsourcing movement are now bringing many of their IT services back in-house.

In the article "9 IT Outsourcing Trends to Watch in 2013" (*CIO,* December 18, 2012), Stephanie Overby notes that outsourcing pioneer GM made the biggest backsourcing splash in 2012, with its announcement that it would bring 10,000 jobs back in-house in coming years. In this article, Steve Martin, partner with outsourcing consultancy Pace Harmon predicted explains why other IT organizations may follow this lead:

"Due to a variety of factors, chief among them the realization that some services are better entrusted to employees rather than 'outsiders,' dissatisfaction with vendor performance, and continued erosion of offshore/onshore rate arbitrage benefits, companies will repatriate currently outsourced infrastructure and in some cases, application development services, at a greater pace."

What's most important to remember is that when companies discover that the financial benefits of their outsourcing deals are dwindling, simply backsourcing may also not be the best solution. Instead, companies may need to rebalance sourcing options to find the optimum blend and rely on third parties only when they can provide a distinct value.

Generally speaking, companies that are backsourcing tend to continue outsourcing for only low-level services — a strategy consistent with (although not necessarily indicative of) value-based IT.

When are the stakes for outsourcing too high? A key example are companies with large ERP systems that support critical business processes. A company implementing or managing large-scale ERP environments has tens or sometimes hundreds of millions of dollars in play. When projects and services of this scale do not succeed, simply removing and replacing vendors doesn't solve underlying problem. In light of the dollars at stake, companies can no longer afford to turn over the reins of their complex ERP environment to industry experts.

Profit-based IT strategies are the common denominator among these project and operational failures. To prevent these failures, companies need to replace the revolving door of consulting firms, vendors, products, and services with analysis, which will enable companies to understand the underlying factors causing IT failures.

Shifting to Value-Based IT

Over the last decade, a myriad of new best practices for managing IT operations and projects has emerged. However, failures and costs continue to increase because these practices don't take into consideration the complete IT ecosystem and dependencies. Further, a 21st century IT organization is now an intricate web of interconnecting and interacting parts whose health is heavily influenced both by internal and external factors, both human and physical.

Companies must avoid the temptation of approaching IT strategy as purely a financial problem to solve and the workforce as commodities that are expendable. In value-based IT, companies focus on outcomes instead of costs.

This emphasis on outcomes isn't a new idea. In the early 1900s, Henry Ford aimed to create an automobile that middle-class Americans could afford. To do that, Ford not only applied assembly-line techniques to manufacturing cars, but also astonished the world by raising his employees' wages to $5 per day, more than doubling the pay for most of his workers. Ford's approach was value-based because, rather than looking solely at costs, Ford connected his desire to sell more cars to his employees' success. In Ford's case, he invested not only in efficient systems, but also in turning his workforce into potential customers who could afford a car. Had Ford looked only at expenses, he wouldn't have seen the potential for expanding his business and his employees' fortunes. For Ford, the move proved extremely profitable. In addition to expanding his customer base, Ford avoided constant turnover, attracted the best mechanics in Detroit, raised productivity, and lowered training costs.

In the same spirit, a value-based approach — in which the *customer* (not profit) drives a departments goals and employee rewards — needs to revolutionize the IT industry. Companies win when the focus is on providing value versus saving money. This requires basing goals, objectives, and rewards on a clear understanding of the customer's need and value proposition for the goods and services provided.

Because a value-based approach makes companies and employees more accountable for outcomes, companies can avoid the rigorous oversight and short-term thinking that characterizes "cheaper, faster, better." Instead, a value-based approach changes how information flows through an organization. In this book, I call the steps for transforming IT the Six Protocols of IT Transformation. These protocols provide the common language and processes that enable IT organizations to drive the right behaviors and achieve desired outcomes.

In summary, the increasing statistics around failed projects, outsourcing, and employee dissatisfaction leaves little room for argument that the current trajectory of IT is trending in the wrong direction. Further, no magic beans or fairy dust (such as the "cheaper, faster, better" approaches) can reverse these trends. This book takes the reader on a journey of how real and sustainable IT transformation can happen in IT organizations.

With the right focus, clarity, motives, measurements, and communication, organizations organically adapt to any transformation successfully. However, the company's transformation must create a culture where employees share a common language, clarify what employees need to do, and base rewards on real outcomes. But before this transformation can happen, a company's leadership must see the world through the eyes of the company's workforce.

PART I

THE PROBLEMS WITH "CHEAPER, FASTER, BETTER"

CHAPTER 1

EXPLORING THE Os OF PROFIT-BASED IT

The Os of profit-based IT do not refer to zeros, although they could because profit-based models are often undermined by project failures, doubled budgets, and backsourcing expenses that zero out any cost savings. Also, as you will discover in this chapter, when an IT initiative begins with the underlying assumptions of profit-based thinking, the IT project often fails, and a ground zero is considered the starting point for rebuilding the IT strategy.

What I really mean by the Os is *objectives, outcomes,* and *ownership.*

In a profit-based IT model, the objective is, of course, profit — often to the exclusion of all else. This focus on profit is understandable: Companies growing their revenues, customer base, users, and transactional volumes are feeling the pressure to reduce costs amid sinking return on assets, intense competition, and changing workforce dynamics. So companies search for the Holy Grail to deliver IT solutions and services faster with higher quality while spending less. They employ outside consulting firms, managed services, and/or software vendors to architect strategies that keep IT budgets flat or even reduce cost. IT organizations then embark on transformational journeys, entrusting their future to outside services that also suffer from the same pressures to reduce costs, increase revenues (billable hours/sales), and increase profits.

However, these profit-based objectives drive unintended outcomes. Employees in the trenches are acutely aware of how companies launch large-scale IT transformation initiatives, including outsourcing, only to find that the company's flexibility and ability to scale is not improved, IT costs are not reduced, and service levels actually drop. When this happens, questions about who owns the problem arise — but only after the consultants have left the building, the employees with institutional knowledge of the business have been laid off or become overwhelmed or disengaged, and the company is left holding third-party agreements that don't reward the services provider for taking ownership of the problems. However, those multimillion-dollar outsourcing deals aren't easily scrapped due the pre-nuptial agreements, and, as noted in the Introduction, backsourcing further disrupts operations and adds to the financial burden. There is an old saying, *"Le bon marché sortir cher,"* or "The cheap comes out expensive."

To understand the benefit of value-based IT, it's important to look at how profit-based IT transformations begin with profit-based objectives, and how these objectives create the environment in which many large-scale IT projects fail.

What's Wrong with Profit-Based Objectives?

For some IT organizations, finding the balance between cost and value is a Sisyphean task. That is, push a stone uphill (reduce costs), watch it roll downhill (decrease value proposition), and then push it up again (reduce costs).

All Information Technology organizations go through cycles where the pendulum swings. Customers and C-level management feel IT costs too much so organizations attempt to drive down costs until the level of service degrades. This incites the business partners and/or external customers to complain and threaten to seek other sources for the IT services. Then budgets are increased, and the pendulum swings back to focus on customer satisfaction (value) because IT is now able to justify the needed budgets. Of course, company leadership soon forgets why they increased IT budgets, and within 3-5 years, the cycle begins again to reduce costs.

To avoid a constantly swinging IT strategy, companies need to change the way they define their objectives, measure outcomes, and create ownership (accountability). Instead of aiming to boost profit in the short term, company leadership needs to change the reward framework. Sustainable transformation occurs when a series of small or moderate changes are made over time, and real long-term benefits (value) are the accumulation of these changes.

The problem is that it's difficult to build a business case for a value-based approach when scorecard objectives and personal rewards are based on short term goals and leaders are only looking at a 6-12 month window for savings. There is no reward for funding investments that benefit one's successor two to four years from now. This mindset fuels the profit-based paradigm driving the beliefs, assumptions, values, and practices that constitute the way the organization views reality.

In other words, what is driving this trend of "cheaper, faster, better" is the desire to drive down the cost of IT without considering the value to the client or customer experience and employee welfare. Furthermore, when these misguided initiatives do not work as expected, rather than correcting the course, companies continue to architect additional controls, oversight, metrics, contract modifications, and layoffs in an attempt to realize the promised savings.

The most important question to ask

What is the problem we are trying to solve?

When this question is answered incorrectly, misguided objectives can destabilize the IT population, reduce productivity, increase development and support expenditures, and cost the organization its most valuable assets: high-performing employees. This question, when answered correctly, can help companies develop a clear IT strategy that transforms the value of IT by leading teams to translate strategic goals into tactical IT solutions.

To get the answer right, business analysis is required. Performing business analysis is the art of applying a research discipline to identifying business needs, gathering requirements, and architecting strategic solutions for the organization to solve business problems.

In *Fourth Generation Management*, author Brian L. Joiner suggests that organizations must be understood and managed as a system, while developing process thinking, making decisions on customer data and understanding the theory of variation.

This means company leadership cannot answer these nine words correctly when they don't ask the right questions. To properly diagnose a problem or recommend a solution, business analysis must include fully understanding the current (as-is) business process so the status quo can be challenged if needed. Ideally, the business analyst or consultant architecting the solution should live a day in the life of the client (whether external to IT or IT itself, such as project teams, PMO, support, and so on).

Business analysts might spend a day with customer care on the phone in the call center, with credit and collections teams to process payments, or with FP&A to go through a month-end close process. Joiner calls this exercise "the check" and it is used to uncover things companies would just as soon not want to know. Further, the check forces companies to look and expose huge wastes in their activities including non-productive things done unknowingly for years that add little value.

In other words, large-scale IT projects are failing not because companies are building the wrong solutions, but because they're getting the problem wrong in the first place. Therefore, getting the problem right can provide a game-changing innovation both for the company and an industry.

Konica cameras: A case study in answering the question

In a Konica Camera case study published in 2012, Sean Gates explores the work of Dr. Takanori Yoneyama to develop Konica's user-friendly cameras in the 1970s. Gates first explains, "If customer satisfaction is your primary purpose, your measurement has to begin and end with the customer. The first stage of this journey is to understand your customers' needs and desires. Surprisingly this is not always as easy as it sounds. What does the customer want?"

In this case, the problem to solve was that Konica wanted to increase market share in the consumer camera market. But, when they talked to the customers, everyone said they were either satisfied with the product or could only suggest minor improvements. To overcome this roadblock to growth, Dr. Yoneyama made this suggestion:

"Perhaps we are asking the wrong questions. We ask for feedback on our camera, but people don't purchase our camera in order to own a camera. They buy a camera in order to take pictures. We see ourselves as manufacturing and selling cameras. Customers see us as a source for acquiring the ability to take pictures. Perhaps we should start seeking feedback on the pictures."

Changing the question and the source for the answers was the turning point in Konica's history. By investigating complaints instead of asking customers what new functionality they wanted, engineers discovered that the main problem was that the pictures customers received back from development had problems with focus, exposure, or superimposed images. When asked about this, customers had a common, different response. "Your camera is great, but I guess I am not a good photographer." Based on this data and feedback, Konica knew it needed to develop cameras that didn't rely on the photographer's skill to take good pictures.

Today, features like auto-focus, auto-exposure, and auto-flash are standard camera features; Konica pioneered these capabilities. The key was asking the right question, which was, "How do we make a better camera?" In IT organizations, the business analyst is the person who asks the right questions and determines the problem to solve.

Good objectives drive good analysis

After you have the right business problem, the next questions are

- Can we solve it?
- Do we have the capability (software, hardware, and experts) to design solutions and meet customer demand?
  - If not, what needs to change in order to do this?
  - If we can provide the new service or offering, can our systems, IT services, and staffing (skills) provide scale to support this?

For example, if IT deploys a new capability or module like Financial Supply Chain Management (FSCM) for credit and collections, can the existing systems support the transactional volumes of credit notes and credit related documents? Do teams understand the FSCM module, and does the IT department have the skills to implement the workflow, soft reminder emails, or web pay features? Is IT positioned to proactively recommend how to enhance this module to help bring business strategies to fruition or drive higher productivity?

What's Wrong with Profit-Based Outcomes?

Whether developing the blueprint for a project or an IT transformation, a company must fully understand the desired outcomes and measurements of the improved condition. To begin, look at the value proposition, define actions needed to accomplish goals, and *then* develop the cost and revenue matrix to implement the project. In other words, do not start with costs analysis, start with defining objectives and expected outcomes.

When the value proposition (instead of profit) drives a project, you can better pinpoint when the cost and profit objectives limit the range of possible outcomes. As illustrated in the Introduction, if Henry Ford had focused solely on cost and profit, he wouldn't have seen how raising employee wages could help expand his business. Similarly, if Konica let profit instead of its customers drive change in the business, Konica wouldn't have had the flexibility and resources to drive innovation in the market.

> When profit is driving outcomes, the focus becomes mitigating the collateral damage to clients and employees to achieve the profit-based goals rather than on providing value.

One way to avoid the collateral damage issue altogether is by asking, "Who benefits from the proposed approach? Is it the IT workforce, the client, or someone else (such as management)?"

Chapter 2 takes a more detailed look at ITIL and ITSM, Agile, and outsourcing and how profit- versus value-based objectives lead to desired or undesirable outcomes for the business.

What Happens to Ownership in a Profit-Based Model?

Unfortunately, a profit-based perspective often leads many companies to believe they can get "cheaper, faster, better" through a painless transition to the new service provider. However, they soon realize the role internal employees play(ed) was not fully understood in the day-to-day operations for keeping the lights on as well as delivering value to the business. Because a profit-based motive is driving the transformation, the company underestimates the value of the internal or tribal knowledge, commitment, and collaboration that comes from having skin in the game.

The problems companies need to solve transcend ITIL, ITSM, Agile, and outsourcing. The solution must balance the growth of IT while ensuring ownership at all levels for the outcomes. Companies cannot just look at outsourcing, delivery/support processes, workforce, or other aspects of this IT problem in verticals or silos.

> Before an IT project or transformation begins, companies need to consider ownership of the outcomes. Unfortunately, profit-based models discourage companies from considering how consulting agreements, transition plans, and budgets can be structured to improve ownership of the outcomes and thus improve the chances that the IT endeavor will succeed.

The following sections take a closer look at how profit-based objectives can create confusion around ownership as an IT project or transformation progresses.

Consulting partners don't own the outcome

There is an undeniable trend of hiring consultants from one's past or for a recognizable name, such as Deloitte, PWC, McKinsey, Accenture, or IBM. Introducing a consulting firm before C-level executives is easier if that consulting firm has a brand and track record. Although brand-name consultants cost more, the consultant's reputation can insulate company leadership from accountability for the failure of the IT transformation, IT project, or new IT service offering.

There is a psychology behind using a brand name because when employees know you are paying top dollar for top consulting services, trust and commitment go up. Unfortunately, so does the price of the IT project: These consulting and/or software firms bill their resources from $200 to $400 or more per hour. However, if the value being provided is not commensurate with perceived costs, internal employees become frustrated and less willing to provide input needed to design the new processes and drive commitment for adoption.

When companies hire consultants to run an IT transformation, they often hand over to consultants the responsibility and accountability for solving IT problems. The problem is that upselling additional goods and services drives the consultant's revenues and success, which conflicts with the consultant's goal of improving the company's condition. When a company depends on consultants to solve internal problems and deliver transformational services, this is a risky position because the consultants may benefit from proposed savings instead of actual improved outcomes and move on before any savings are realized or quantified.

To protect the investment in consulting services and the IT project overall, accountability and responsibility for shaping the vision and strategy must remain in-house. Rather than relying on consultants to drive a whole project or transformation, a company can use consultants' expertise to shorten the horizon for developing and implementing new strategies or technologies. The real expertise needed to transform IT and ensure alignment must come from those who understand the critical business processes, technology landscape, and competencies required to support the business growth.

A company (client) also needs to have defined outcomes so that any agreement made with a consulting firm can reflect those outcomes. A client can structure consulting services using a value-based approach instead of a straight T&M (time and materials) model, including a fixed cost or an earn-out model over two years based on outcomes. For example, Statement of Works (SOWs) on a large implementation should be tied in part to tangible savings realized (return on investment) or successful delivery of *all* agreed-upon functionality. Most consulting firms prefer purely T&M engagements over fixed or commission-based fee structures, because T&M doesn't enable clients to seek remedies (money back) if the firm does not successfully meet the objectives. The agreement is focused on physical bodies or boots on the ground billing in time units. Under these agreements, vendors can easily point to internal problems (real or imagined) as being responsible for the failed outcomes.

In *Control Your ERP Destiny*, author Steven Scott Phillips describes how organizations must educate themselves to understand what ownership looks like and implement strategies to assume increased control of their projects. He explains that far too often, consultants blame clients for not taking ownership of IT strategies and ERP projects. Phillips points out then ". . . consultants should be advising clients on the importance of taking ownership of their own ERP implementation in the beginning of any engagement." The author goes on to explain that companies assume risk when a software or consulting firm has little interest in truly educating and teaching companies how to become more self-reliant, because this self-reliance would conflict with creating more billable hours and increasing revenues. Even when vendors have the best intentions for the client, ownership becomes a matter of the consultant's individual style and personal ethics.

IT budgets limit ownership

A profit-based IT strategy typically aims to drive down costs, increase throughput, and increase quality all at the same time. However, these objectives are out of touch with reality. Companies simply cannot sustain ongoing growth of their customer base, users, and transactional volumes while expecting to spend less every year (year-over-year). Also IT can't achieve same the predictable outcomes delivered in the past when demand for services is going up and headcount is being reduced or replaced with cheaper and less skilled workers.

For example, in a profit-based model, say that a business triples its revenues, users, customers, and suppliers during a four-year period. In addition, the business requires new functionality to support growth around pricing, credits, collections, financials, and/or distribution services. Although the number one priority on the company scorecard is to grow the business and take market share, the company works against its objective by keeping IT budgets flat year-over-year, while expecting IT to reduce costs and increase scale. Further, IT scorecard objectives may ask teams to increase operational efficiencies on top of the budget constraints. However, in this scenario, increasing efficiencies isn't possible because most IT employees are heads-down trying to keep the lights on and support the business (with a white glove service model everyone expects). In the end, the IT department simply doesn't have the bandwidth to move the dial on operational efficiencies.

Moreover, when organizations reduce investments in IT assets (hardware/software) to save money, such as postponing software upgrades, hardware refreshes, implementation of new modules and capabilities, this has long-term impacts for robust and scalable IT solutions. With each postponement, the cost of IT increases exponentially. When IT can't take advantage of new capabilities or ERP modules, employees often need to write custom code that handles an issue or the business need until the system can be upgraded. The unintended outcome is that upgrades require exhaustive testing of custom code, which adds to the overall cost.

The upshot is that profit-based models simply do not enable IT to take ownership of the services IT provides. In a value-based model, IT organizations and their budgets are scaled relative to growth. Scaling the budget still controls costs, but reduces the number of failed projects, repeat incidents, and outages. Scaling the budget also positions IT to quickly adapt services as the business landscape changes.

Employees struggle to take ownership

As Chapter 2 will explain, IT trends such as ITIL, ITSM, and Agile come with a set of best practices that may be used selectively to support a profit-based model. When this happens, employees are seen as interchangeable and must follow rigid protocols in an effort to systematically handle simple and complex tasks alike. The unintended outcome is that employees are stripped of autonomy to innovate when handling support issues or small enhancements on behalf of the IT customers. Further, when project teams morph into scrum teams, they often lose the support and vision of a dedicated and qualified project manager. As a result, projects lack someone who provides oversight and is accountable for the overall outcomes (cradle to grave). In both cases, employees aren't able to take ownership of outcomes, even if they want to.

Even if the IT project or transformation uses a value-based model, employees will still need help managing a transition in order to take ownership of (or buy in to) the company's new system and structures. After the strategy is decided, managing change is just as important when successfully executing any transformation, because it's not just the technology and processes that undergo the change. People are going through a transition.

Culture and transparency can significantly improve adoption of organizational change and employee commitment to execute on the change.

Employees do not have to agree with the approach. They just need to understand the connection between the strategy and the desired outcomes. If value-based motives drive the outcomes, employees can align with those outcomes in order to improve the company and IT client's condition. In contrast, when motives are profit-driven, such as reducing IT costs to hit short-term financial targets for the purposes of bonuses and stock options, real alignment is not possible. When employees don't trust that the employer's motives are aligned with the stated company objectives, employees become disengaged and apathetic.

CHAPTER SUMMARY

Before embarking on an IT project or IT transformation, especially a large one, companies need to weigh cost versus value.

- **Start by answering the question, "What is the problem we are trying to solve?"** To find the right answers, make sure the answer addresses for whom IT is creating value and how. Let customers and IT's end-product or services, rather than the company's balance sheet, take center stage.

- **Use the objectives to define the desired outcomes.** The proposed delivery, services, and operations framework should support the value proposition IT brings. As will be explained in Chapter 2, this framework may include leveraging key partnerships where some activities are outsourced or require resources outside of the enterprise. This also may require new standard processes like ITIL or ITSM, or may not.

- **Don't let consultants and profit-based objectives overshadow the question of who takes ownership of the IT project's outcomes.** Managing customer relationships and expectations is essential. Company leadership needs to identify and motivate all the key resources (human assets) required to deliver on all commitments made.

- **Make sure metrics and rewards account for who needs to take ownership of the outcomes.** A company needs to take a holistic approach that considers all factors, including the IT workforce, business partners, IT management, and organizational culture.

ANALYZING IT TRENDS AND BELIEF SYSTEMS

Behind any trend is a belief driving people to adopt that trend.

This chapter looks at underlying beliefs about IT trends — namely outsourcing IT services to third-party vendors, ITIL/ITSM processes, and Agile development — because understanding these belief systems helps reveal what does and doesn't work in implementing these trends.

What's wrong (or right) with these trends? Well, it depends on who you ask. Often, the IT client, IT worker, IT vendor, IT manager, and IT senior leader are like the five blind men and an elephant. The elephant's keeper tells the men, "This is an elephant," and each develops a different conception of what an elephant is, based on the part of the elephant they touch.

After each has touched a different part of the elephant, the blind men continue down the road, arguing vehemently as they go about what an elephant is like, each believing that he, and he alone, is right and the others are wrong. Sound familiar?

Similarly, employees and customers of IT have belief systems that affect their perspective and willingness to adapt to the changing IT landscape around them. Unfortunately, large companies rarely have the patience of this imagined elephant that tolerates a bunch of blind men touching its legs and ears and pulling on its tail, as each attempts to figure out what the elephant is — or in the company's case, how belief systems are unconsciously affecting the groundwork and objectives for a large-scale IT project or transformation.

Belief is a state of the mind in which a subject regards a thing to be true. A *belief system* is a set of powerful convictions, sometimes with far-reaching psychological implications. When belief systems are in conflict, resolving the conflict can be difficult. To begin resolving this conflict, first you must understand what the current belief is. Then find a way to reduce the certainty of the belief. This chapter examines and confutes some of the belief systems responsible for the trends and failures in IT organizations. Also replaces those beliefs with new ones including backing this up with credible supporting data.

Understanding How Technological Change Has Impacted Beliefs about IT Trends

Over the past 20 years, the information technology industry has undergone a metamorphosis. The landscape for technology, process, and people looks very different than it did two decades ago. At that time, digital cellular technology did not exist, Microsoft operating systems and Intel hardware were in their infancy, and commercial websites were still a novelty. As the technology landscape rapidly changed, companies like SAP, Oracle, and PeopleSoft raced to take market share for ERP Software Applications using a new client–server (two-tier) approach. Even then, technology was changing our way of life.

However, technology and software changed more than just the delivery of IT solutions. Company cultures, staffing strategies, values, and priorities changed, too — driven by the belief that to remain competitive in a global marketplace, companies must adapt IT strategies to drive down costs. Business leaders came to believe that companies need to adopt best practices like ITSM, ITIL, Agile, and outsourcing for project delivery and operations, or else their companies would get left behind.

Consequently, today, more than ever, IT organizations find themselves in a constant state of change, always looking for new cost-saving measures. IT organizations are caught in seemingly never-ending cycles of transformation, never really taking the time to step back and consider whether the implementation of these IT trends is working.

When IT initiatives and projects fail to deliver on their expected outcomes, companies point to the consultants, outsourcing vendors, and delivery strategies for the failed projects and operations, rather than recognize that the company itself set the stage for these failures by basing the strategy on profit-based outcomes and/or by not effectively managing transformations. Looking outward is easier than looking in the mirror.

You have wonder, at some point, after you hired the best consultants money can buy, fired all the low performers, implemented the industry best practices for operations and projects, and outsourced to the top managed service provider, what are you missing?

Until companies perform forensic analysis to pinpoint root causes for IT failures (such as problems with service levels, ongoing cost issues, and so on), companies can't say with certainty whether the outside services hired, methodologies adopted, implementation itself, or company culture caused the project failures.

The Outsourcing Conundrum

Gartner research estimates that, around the world, over 30 leading outsourcing locations are spread across the Americas, Asia, Central and Eastern Europe, Africa, and the Middle East. According to a 2013 study by Statistic Brain, 43 percent of technology companies in the U.S. outsource, which accounts for nearly 2,637,239 U.S. jobs sent offshore. The number one reason for outsourcing is reducing costs, as shown in Figure 2-1, which reflects the numbers from the Statistic Brain study.

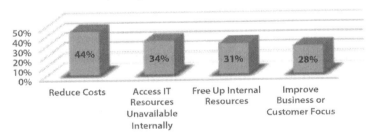

Figure 2-1

Companies continue to attempt to drive down the total cost of ownership (TCO) for Enterprise IT by outsourcing work to managed service vendors. A broad matrix of categories and KPIs (key performance indicators) are used to select the best vendor to mitigate risks. Outsourcing is a big investment not taken lightly, and the benefits of outsourcing are hard to argue with. According to marketing materials and industry beliefs, IT outsourcing can give the business the power to leverage shared human assets, driving increased productivity and a higher bottom line. Managed services can provide everything so companies can concentrate on what is really important, such as the following:

- Core company activities
- Cost and efficiency savings
- Reduced overhead and better operational controls
- Staffing flexibility and scalability
- Continuity and risk management
- Internal staff development

An added benefit of outsourcing is that the client does not have to interview or vet individual resources to join the teams, unlike full-time employees. Companies also do not have to manage employee payroll or other administrative costs of outsourced jobs. The vendor provides employee on- and off-boarding. In fact, managed service providers handle finding, interviewing, hiring, retaining, and firing of all talent required to support the operations and project delivery IT services, at an agreed-upon price. Not only is this a big savings for IT, but also for HR and other corporate services supplied by internal employees.

Keep in mind that savings are not realized in the first or second year, because the transition to a managed service provider typically requires a one-time balloon investment amortized over five years. The company has to pay for things like involuntary separation packages, placement services for jobs outsourced, and costs for knowledge transfer including shadowing of internal employees. Fine-tuning master service agreements and modifying contracts for services not spelled out right the first time often result in additional, unforeseen expenses. Costs resulting from responsibilities shifting, restructuring, and decision support tools for workforce, portfolio and release management also increase the total cost of ownership (TCO) for outsourcing. These inherent costs includes new standard operating procedures, implementation costs for new system development lifecycles (SDLC) and/or ITIL processes, and training for all these changes. Finally, the company needs to pay for new employees who implement the vendor management program, oversee the master service agreement (MSA), and generate cyclic analytics for contract administration.

To accurately calculate the TCO of outsourcing, companies must consider direct and indirect costs and their ripple effect to the business in achieving their goals, including missed return on investment (ROI) for project commitments delayed by the transition.

Assuming the transition to managed services is successful, the next problem arises when talented resources leave the vendor or lower-skilled off-shore workers gain new skills and ultimately move on to more lucrative opportunities. The managed service provider is left in the position of back-filling or rotating resources between client sites and training replacements. This causes reduced service levels and long hours for those remaining.

Another consideration is that off-shore now pops up in new countries, offering even lower costs, thereby creating more competition for cheaper labor. If companies use price point (profit-based criteria) to drive the vendor selection, they are likely to change to cheaper provider when their contracts end, incurring conversion costs yet again.

Most importantly, like the clients they serve, outsourcing companies also seek the highest profit margins achievable with the lowest cost structure. This places the vendor in the same dilemma as the client: how to deliver IT services while consistently driving down costs and increasing profits? On the face of it, this presents a conflict of interest. Vendor account representatives and executives are rewarded for the deals they sign, the revenue they generate, and profitability for each engagement, while reducing the costs to provide outsourcing services. Vendors, like their clients, are constantly looking for ways to drive economy of scale while reducing internal operational expenditures (OPEX) for supporting each account. In addition, most consulting firms and managed services give their employees incentives for increasing the scope of work, costs, and billable hours. In other words, the service provider has goals to generate more revenue from existing accounts while simultaneously finding new ways to fulfill existing commitments at a lower cost.

If clients are willing to trade higher-skilled, higher-paid, long-term employees for lower-skilled workers to drive down costs, managed service providers likely do the same, effectively making workers commodities who can be easily replaced and are therefore paid less.

In summary, to avoid the perils of what author Seth Godin calls PERL (percentage of easily replaced labors, a concept discussed in more detail in the upcoming section on ITIL), an outsourcing assessment cannot just focus on a managed service provider's brand, location, time-zone, or costs. Other value-based factors carry equal weight in the scoring, such as the following:

- Attrition rates
- Communications
- Cultural compatibility
- Infrastructure
- Internal methodology for delivering IT services

For example, when the client retains experienced in-house business ana-lysts writing clear requirements and technical specifications using a water-fall delivery method (define, design, build/test, prepare for production, and go-live), then the need for frequent communications in the same time zone may not be as critical. If the client uses an Agile development model (con-ceive, prototype, develop, and release) that requires daily interaction, these factors (communication and time zone) may be an important consideration for choosing location. In both cases the cultural compatibility for the orga-nization may be critical to success. For example, do the resources need to be more assertive when working with the customers (internal and exter-nal)? Can the vendor adapt their communication and engagement style to the culture of the client to ensure optimum results? Although the number one reason for outsourcing is reducing costs, perhaps this is the reason over 50 percent of these engagements are failing.

The Backsourcing Phenomenon

In the 2013 *CIO* article, "Companies Retake the Reins on IT Services," Howard Baldwin describes how many high-profile companies like Chase and GM are backsourcing: "Companies have been cancelling major outsourcing deals as long as there have been major outsourcing deals — indications are there is a shift in thinking underway."

Charles Green, a Forrester Research analyst, noted "an ongoing level of dis-satisfaction with outsourcing," citing a 2012 services survey of some 1,000 IT services professionals, in which nearly half the respondents listed poor service quality as a challenge and 32 percent stated they were looking to bring work back in-house.

Some believe that backsourcing is a growing phenomenon, and all agree it comes with significant implications for organizations, including managing organizational change, restructuring, reintegrating knowledge, rehiring employees, and re-establishing in-house capabilities and expertise in critical business processes. Unfortunately, companies cannot outsource the backsourcing effort, and usually when backsourcing begins, a company has limited in-house knowledge about how to successfully accomplish the backsourcing transition. Further, unless companies have maintained a sig-nificant footprint of full-time employees, the transition lowers service levels and delays projects.

The key to a successful backsourcing initiative is getting alignment across the organization for the change. This means working closely with the IT teams and IT clients to develop a shared success model, thereby generating the needed momentum to ride out the painful waves of transition on the promise of a brighter future for all.

ITIL and ITSM: The Theory Versus Reality

"Cheaper, faster, better" can come in many forms. Although outsourcing is normally associated with a profit-based strategy to control costs, Information Technology Infrastructure Library (ITIL) and IT service management (ITSM) must also be considered. Keep in mind, ITIL, ITSM and outsourcing themselves are not the problem, it is the profit-based motives driving the strategy of how to use and integrate these solutions into the company. In a nutshell, ITIL are the set of practices focused on aligning IT services with the needs of the business. So far so good, this sounds like a value-based principle.

However, ITIL's goal is to provide a discipline to establish processes, procedures, tasks, and checklists (not organization-specific), that can be integrated into the organization's strategy to deliver value while *maintaining a minimum level of competency*. In other words, its function is to show the company how to document everything done in IT so the lowest skilled laborer can use this documentation to perform IT work, thereby reducing costs. Here is where the problem lies.

This idea is perpetuated by a modern myth that the business you own should be able to serve as prototype for more just like it. Further, this is only possible when everything performs like a repeatable system. In fact, you should be able to hand the how-to manual to just anyone to do a task as well as anyone else. Through this model, the myth promises, operational costs are reduced and labor is cheaper because employees need to possess only the lowest level of skill necessary to fulfill the functions for which they are intended. This is how McDonald's revolutionized the restaurant industry and changed farming and food distribution businesses in the 1950s by developing a Speedee Service System of food preparation. In this business model, the workforce is reduced to a commodity or what the author Seth Godin refers to as Percent of Easily Replaced Laborers (PERL). Godin says, "If you create a cookie-cutter company filled with rules and procedures that are designed to allow hiring cheap people, you will have to produce a product without humanity, personalization, or connection. Which means you will have to lower prices to compete, that leads to a race to the bottom."

This has worked for some retail business models. For example, Burger King was an outgrowth of McDonald's as was Pizza Hut, Taco Bell, and KFC. The business model was not organization-specific so it was easily replicated. Today, fast food chains use price-point to attract customers versus quality. However, information technology is not a retail business model.

The good news is, reducing the skill level required to perform the task is only half of the equation in ITIL. The methodology also promises to improve operations by establishing baselines so organizations can plan, implement, and measure the value of IT services as well as demonstrate compliance and measure improvement. In fact, the intent of ITIL was to create a holistic perspective, end to end, on the full life cycle of services needed to deliver IT to the customer.

For example, the IT Financial Management discipline promotes that IT infrastructure and services be provided at the most effective price — which does not necessarily mean cheapest. This discipline should be used as a tool for calculating the cost of providing IT services so organizations can recover these costs from the customer. Today, most companies cherry-pick ITIL practices in an effort to purely reduce costs and ignore those ITIL offerings that do not align with profit-based motives. This is not to say ITIL/ITSM does not work, but when used this way, it cannot drive long-term benefits. ITIL and outsourcing must blend into the organization so parts are indistinguishable to the business, IT shared services, managed services, and the dedicated IT workforce. Simply put, ITIL must be holistically considered and seamlessly integrated.

ITIL originated as a collection of books, each covering a specific practice within ITSM and built around a process-model view of controlling and managing operations. At the center of the ITIL Service Lifecycle is the Service Strategy, providing guidance on clarification and prioritization of service-provider investments. Service Strategy focuses on helping IT organizations improve and develop over the long term. ITIL volumes cover the following key areas:

1. IT service management

2. Service portfolio management

3. Financial management for IT services

4. Demand management

5. Business relationship management

In a 2006 online Baseline Magazine interview about IT management, Ed Holub, a Gartner analyst who fields 500 inquiries a year from different clients related to ITIL, explains ITIL this way:

"ITIL is a set of integrated, best practice process guidance that focuses on the core service delivery and service support processes that any IT infrastructure and operations organization performs. ITIL is high-level and focuses on what should be done, but doesn't describe at a detailed level how to do it. The goal of ITIL is to transform an organization to be more process and service-centric by changing the culture of an organization to embrace the value inherent in standardization versus one-off solutions."

In other words, industry ITIL best practices advocate that organizations reduce all IT service offerings to a set of common practices, thereby removing all one-off solutions in IT.

However, most companies tend to implement ITIL practices selectively and usually only those practices related to driving down costs. An inherent risk of ITIL is that organizations and consultants take the content of the books literally and try to implement processes, roles, and functions exactly as described in documentation. This, coupled with underlying profit-based motives, results in underfunding the one-time investment needed to properly develop a flexible framework, document processes in standard operating procedures, provide change leadership, configure and implement tools, and roll-out effective training. In some cases, staff are expected to work in both models (old and new) for an extended period of time during transition, further straining the limited resource capacity and reducing commitment to — and adoption of — the new approach.

For architects attempting to transform the organization with ITIL/ITSM and Agile, creating a one-size-fits-all approach isn't easy, because the processes that IT teams follow vary from area to area. For example, consider the following issues:

- Developing customer-facing applications with compliance standards for open source code, ICD10, and HIPPA is approached much differently than internal infrastructure services or ERP systems for internal users like distribution, financials, accounts payable, and accounts receivable.
- Even within the ERP landscape, delivery processes and workflow vary widely. B2B, EDI, BI, and customer portals don't always follow the same approach or delivery strategy.

Although adopting an ITIL framework can increase the speed to market in some cases, the adoption must be approached using a value-based mindset. Identify desired business or IT outcomes, identify actions that need to happen, decide what investments the organization is willing to make, and align rewards with outcomes. In the *Baseline* interview, Ed Holub advocates a similar value-based approach to ITIL, stating that,

> "It is important to select a balanced set of metrics to gauge the health of processes from both an efficiency and effectiveness perspective. If either efficiency (cost) or effectiveness (quality) is overemphasized you may inadvertently drive the wrong behavior."

Moreover, how an ITIL framework is adopted isn't all that matters. Equally important is why a company is making the change. What is the problem the company is trying to solve?

When employees perceive profit-based motives are driving the methodology and strategy to deliver IT solutions and services, employees struggle to commit to and adopt the new solutions. In some cases, those forced to adopt these practices know the new practices may mean the end of their jobs. When employees are motivated by fear, they don't address or improve the problems they see in the new processes, hoping that the entire initiative will fail and things will return to their former state. In these situations, employees may attend training, follow new practices, go through the motions, and focus on ensuring they have no personal failures. In exchange for their obedience, they receive rewards and compensation independent from the success of the IT transformation.

I might note here that you won't find ITIL and ITSM in startup companies or in companies delivering a new ERP implementation, because ITIL and ITSM repress the enterprising spirit required to take innovative risks and create high-quality and high-value solutions in a short amount of time. The ITIL and ITSM methodologies discourage people from thinking on their feet or working outside standard processes, even when doing so is in the client's best interest. Rather, these frameworks reward compliance with following standard processes.

Agile

In Agile, scrum teams focus on releases rather than on projects. Releases mark a moment of moving functionality that provides a customer new capability. To achieve a release, the scrum team develops in sprints focused on the release objective. Release cycles require comprehensive planning with a wider perspective than just a single scrum team. Release planning is the wider view that is necessary to take a full software release to market successfully.

The popularity of the scrum team model grew from The Agile Manifesto, which is based on 12 principles:

1. Achieve customer satisfaction by delivering useful software rapidly.
2. Welcome changing requirements, even late in development.
3. Deliver working software frequently (weeks rather than months).
4. Developers collaborate with business people closely and daily.
5. Build projects around motivated individuals, who should be trusted.
6. Communicate face-to-face, which is the best form of communication, and work in the same location.

7. Working software is the principal measure of progress.

8. Maintain a constant pace of development.

9. Give ongoing attention to technical excellence and good design.

10. Simplicity — the art of maximizing the amount of work not done — is essential.

11. Teams should be self-organizing.

12. Adapt to changing circumstances regularly.

At face value, Agile principles appear customer centered, promoting a value-driven approach for delivering solutions. Yet in the execution, the release strategy and Agile philosophies are in conflict. For example, Agile welcomes changing requirements, even late in development, but release cycles (or sprints) drive a different behavior. Team members become nervous or even impatient with business partners who want to expand scope or rethink needed functionality. Ideas introduced late into the sprint may not get a fair evaluation and consideration. Therefore, changes are pushed off to another release, resulting in redesign and rework in the future, or the changes are dismissed entirely.

Most self-organizing scrum teams are not actually inclusive of all skill sets needed to deliver on an entire project, nor do the teams always work at the same location, especially when managed services are feathered into the delivery approach. Furthermore, because scrum teams are focused on sprints or Service Design Packages (SDPs) and measured in timeboxes versus projects as a whole, the project often lacks a project manager or someone with accountability for delivering all the agreed-upon functionality, end to end, to the client. Because projects are broken down into SDPs and sprints, the project can be handed off to different scrum teams over time as the project progresses from inception to go-live. Although the manifesto champions value-based outcomes with the client, Agile delivery processes can drive behaviors that are counterproductive.

To deliver software frequently, in weeks rather than months, Agile methods break tasks into small increments and do not fully consider long-term planning and dependencies with other teams. Iterations are mapped to short time frames (timeboxes) that typically last from one to four weeks. Once again, if working software is the goal, the principles and processes conflict with each other, because working software must include the integration testing of all dependencies with other teams, not just unit testing by one scrum team.

A typical Agile project requires that each iteration include cross-functional teams working in concert for all project phases: planning, requirements analysis, design, coding, unit testing, and acceptance testing. At the end of each iteration, a working product is demonstrated to stakeholders. According to Agile theory, this approach minimizes overall risk and allows the project to adapt to changes quickly. Although an iteration might not add enough functionality to warrant a market software release, the goal is to have an available release (with minimal bugs). Keep in mind that multiple iterations might be required to release a product or new features. The principle is that all teams are working together as a single unit to deliver the release.

However, in practice, the introduction of scrum teams creates more verticals, resulting in an unintended dynamic across the teams. Unlike waterfall or ASAP (Accelerated SAP) projects, in which team members are mapped and accountable to a single project manager ultimately responsible for all deliverables, scrum teams focus only on their piece of the work. All teams want to end up wearing the white hat by delivering their functionality in the prescribed timebox with no defects, even at the expense of blaming other teams. Often, coordination becomes the number one delay for cross-functional teams working to complete their individual assignments. The verticals and silos reduce productivity on all teams. Unlike waterfall project teams that operate more like tribes, in the Agile model, the tribe is divided into clans that are territorial versus communal.

In contrast, in a value-based system development life cycle (SDLC) or waterfall approach, the tribe includes the entire project team and spans all capability areas, thereby creating a shared responsibility and accountability for success. Teams are not measured on small increments delivered, and whether the entire solution is delivered in one release or in multiple go-lives makes no difference. The only goal is to deliver on all commitments within the agreed-upon timeframes and costs, unless the client agrees to something else (via change control). Requirements can change, problems arise, and new information becomes available that can alter scope, time, and expected outcomes. In the waterfall approach, the team is aligned behind a common goal, which creates a sense of common purpose, or a tribal culture.

A Profit-Based Case Study

"Cheaper, faster, better" was the tagline used to explain the benefits of ITIL, ITSM, and outsourcing when a Fortune 500 company announced the layoff of 70 percent of its SAP systems operations and project services teams in

2008. However, "cheaper, faster, better" were not three words employees and business partners used to describe the experience. Although this IT transformation used outsourcing and ITIL/ITSM, these strategies weren't to blame. Most IT professionals understand and embrace standard processes for portfolio, demand, and capacity management. They welcome documenting the full life cycle of services for the entire IT organization, including all supporting components needed to deliver services to the customer. Most even agree that outsourcing some tasks — such as running a Test Center of Excellence (TCoE), building regression test libraries, executing test scripts, monitoring systems, and maintaining some security and user support — can be an effective way to save money, because these tasks can be scripted and executed like factory work.

At first glance, the company's SAP department transformation strategy and approach seemed best of class. Top consulting firms were hired to architect the strategy and develop detailed transition plans. ITIL, ITSM, and Agile were adopted to help drive operational efficiencies. A significant amount of knowledge transfer, including employee shadowing, was factored into the transition plan for the new outsourcing managed service vendor. The company made investments in training, tools, and organization restructuring. The company even retained a number of involuntarily separated employees as contractors to ensure a smooth transition, despite the impact to the return on investment (ROI). So what went wrong?

As it turned out, adopting a "cheaper, faster, better" philosophy resulted in unexpected outcomes because the strategy was based on reducing the level of competency required to perform the same jobs. Among the employees who were let go, some employees were performing duties that required skills beyond routine IT work. Furthermore, in areas that lacked enough in-house knowledge and documentation of critical business processes, effective knowledge transfer suffered, or tribal knowledge was lost in translation and transition, because no value-based metrics enabled company leadership to evaluate this activity. Indeed, scorecards focused only on profit-based outcomes, such as creating scale, increasing throughput, reducing costs, or tracking the number of tickets closed.

In addition, the ITIL metrics did not include a way to quantify the indirect costs of missed deliverables, missed timelines, missing functionality, outages, and customer dissatisfaction. As a result, the total cost of ownership did not decrease, the quality of work did not increase, and speed to market did not improve.

In retrospect, three faulty assumptions contributed to the failed approach:

- **Everything needs to be a system. Think of your business as a franchise prototype. You should be able to hand the how-to manual to just anyone.**

  - Some of IT is factory or service catalog work, like setting up new users, adding security roles and permissions, and adding capacity to a server, but not everything can be scripted. In fact, most of the real value that IT provided did not fit easily into an ITSM management tool or service design package. As I explain later in this book, project blueprint and design, repeat incidents, performance issues, and complex projects do not have predictable and scriptable tasks performed in sequence to find solutions. In some cases, the company used ITSM processes to track deliverables that were actually simple change requests (such as applying an OSS note, creating database indexes, or users asking for a new payment method), increasing the overhead for IT and reducing productivity.

  - When the company split the strategy between using an incident/change management and ITSM tools, employees and service providers became confused about when and how to use ITIL/ITSM for day-to-day operations because the processes became very subjective. In this example, employees complained of delays that resulted from ITSM workflow steps and approvals that didn't add value. Seemingly, because the company wanted to architect a one-size-fits-all approach to an ITIL/ITSM implementation, the approach didn't reflect differences across the various IT teams, such as database, EDI, QA, BI, and so on. The methodology required employees to create service design packages (SDPs), user stories, and request for change (RFCs) without considering how to integrate these deliverables with existing system development life cycle (SDLC) requirements still in place for project plans, blueprint/requirements documents, functional/technical specifications, and unit test plans. As a result, teams had to perform redundant tasks, which decreased their efficiency.

- **After IT services and delivery processes are documented, they can be easily transitioned to another service provider.**

  - In this case study, the scorecards didn't reflect the impact of replacing seasoned employees with cheaper workers who are inexperienced with the business processes. Further, the new resources had little or no direct engagement with business partners and, in some cases, rotated between clients. Because the profit-based metrics looked only at the labor costs and didn't factor in the labor's value (that is, cheaper and less experienced workers add costs for rework and additional oversight), the predicted savings for this IT transformation were never realized.

- The ITIL metrics did not compare the old model against the new. For example, in the old model, the business analyst, developer, and business partner worked together directly to solve a problem that prevented multiple iterative cycles of trial and error seen with the offshore model. There was no way to quantify the level of innovation this collaboration fostered as compared to the new ITSM discipline that mechanized processes into workflow events for support and scrum teams. Another assumption was that the business analyst's functional work (configuration) could be performed offshore. However, the time needed to write exhaustive functional specifications, perform configuration reviews, and rework missed requirements trumped any savings.

- **Creating scrum teams and release schedules enables the organization to deliver on commitments with higher quality and certainty.**

  - Using dedicated scrum teams and delivering in 90-day sprints introduced additional oversight by resource and release managers. In the Agile model, the project manager role was decommissioned, and resource managers and scrum leads managed deliverables. The scheduling process using timebox intervals required both resource and release managers to constantly reshuffle commitments throughout the 90 day sprint. The fear of missing the quarterly release date drove undesired behaviors to meet the time and cost constraints at the expense of value for the client.
  - The scrum teams were not inclusive of all skill sets required, such as BASIS (operating system and database), EAI (enterprise application integration), or EDI (electronic data interchange) because those departments operated under a different model for delivery. Also, not all delivery teams (such as major projects or legacy IT systems) adopted ITIL/ITSM, which created more confusion for the scrum teams, shared services team, and release managers who scheduled work across functional areas. As a result, pockets of IT continued to use local SDLCs and other internal processes to deliver projects and enhancements. All IT departments were not able to align with a common language and discipline.

As these examples illustrate, the mistake wasn't adding outsourcing, ITIL/ITSM, and Agile to IT business processes. The mistake was setting objectives based on financial targets versus value. The approach emphasized documenting, standardizing, and automating everyone's job into a prescribed script so those jobs could be delivered with the lowest cost labor. Not enough consideration was made to align IT services with the needs of business or with each other within the IT department. A value-based approach may have also used ITIL/ITSM and outsourcing to improve operational efficiencies, but considered the pitfalls discussed and adjusted the strategy to gain optimum costs versus maximum savings.

Chapter Summary

This chapter explored underlying beliefs about IT trends in an effort to understand these beliefs systems and pinpoint what does and doesn't work in implementing these trends. Here are some key points to take away:

- "Cheaper, faster, better" focuses on reducing costs at any cost by aligning the strategy with profit-based (financial) goals and not considering value-based objectives of improving the client's condition or retaining internal talent.

- When employees are treated like commodities that are interchangeable, IT becomes nothing more than factory work. The commodification of jobs destroys any chance to kindle the flame of innovation that is the catalyst for providing value to the IT client.

- Different technical service centers may require different processes to deliver on their value proposition. When using ITIL, ITSM, and/or Agile for project, portfolio, and workforce management, the processes must be tailored to the needs of each IT team, project, or service area rather than standardized across the organization.

- Keep workflow, tracking, and metrics as light and adaptive as possible. Avoid unnecessary approvals or data collection for metrics that take away time from project team members and provide no actionable intelligence. Only track information in detail when it's necessary for accounting or helps to pinpoint inefficiencies on delivery teams.

- Companies must ensure any ITIL/ITSM tools used do not create redundancy to capture the needed artifacts and approvals required to move change through the environment.

- The delivery framework chosen must call out all dependencies on other teams and how work will move seamlessly through each process. The delivery process must create a sense of shared success and accountability for project and services instead of just rewarding individual teams for hitting their deliverables.

- Outsourcing, ITIL, ITSM, and Agile are not a one-size-fits-all solution for IT. When leveraging vendors and/or methodologies, be clear on the problem that needs to be solved and the motives behind it.

The key is balancing the profit mindset against the value proposition, including accepting less savings in exchange for increased customer satisfaction, higher predictability of outcomes, and improved employee engagement (meaningful jobs).

CHAPTER 3

THE NEXT TECTONIC SHIFT: VALUE-BASED IT

Companies need to be forward-thinking about their IT philosophy, processes, and culture if they are to increase scale while ensuring predictable and repeatable high-quality outcomes. To position IT employees and capabilities for the technological and business challenges of today and the future, companies need to re-engineer the IT landscape through the lens of value-based principles. This includes setting better goals, improving client relationships, making the right investments, and developing rewards that drive new behaviors.

Unfortunately, there are no turnkey solutions that reduce costs and increase productivity. Instead each company needs to architect a unique IT delivery and support organization that is locally owned and relevant to the teams in order to restore a sense of connectedness (teamwork) and gain a competitive advantage. That's what this chapter is all about: understanding the value-based mindset and introducing the first steps toward implementing a value-based IT transformation.

Shifting to a Value-Based Mindset

Before a company's IT leadership begins exploring specific tactics for implementing value-based IT, they need to lay the groundwork for how to cultivate a value-based based mindset. There is no doubt that the profit-based strategies are not working. In contrast, mounting evidence suggests that companies that are taking a value-based approach to their people, processes, and technology consistently outperform those companies using a profit-based model of "cheaper, faster, better."

The primary difference between the two models comes down to focus and philosophy. In the following table, you can see how profit-based thinking is focused on the cost of IT services, operations, and initiatives. In contrast, value-based goals focus on usability, adoption, scalability, and supportability.

TABLE 3-1   Profit-Based Focus versus Value-Based Focus

Profit-Based IT	Value-Based IT
OPEX budgets	Functionality and capabilities
On time, on budget	Usability and adoption
Headcount	Availability and scalability
Rates and costs	Employee engagement
Incidents and defects	Customer engagement

> The success of information technology lies at the crossroads of what clients want or need and what IT teams can deliver. Delivering value requires a shift in focus from the cost of projects and services managed to the needs of the client and users.

The following sections highlight the key strategic principles that support a successful value-based IT transformation.

Employees thrive when they have a clear purpose

The first step in triaging the increasing statistics around IT failures is acknowledging that the value IT delivers isn't just factory work. Real innovation happens and art is created when confusion, fear, and uncertainty are replaced with clarity about what employees are here to do.

Value-based IT helps to provide that clarity by removing silos, unnecessary gates, useless approvals, and workflows that delay project teams, increase employee frustration, and reduce productivity. Value-based IT can also reduce time spent on unnecessary operational and project metrics that do not translate into fewer defects or reaching new service levels of quality.

In other words, employees develop a sense of purpose in their work, because value-based IT minimizes the administrative overhead that can bog down the IT staff's ability to make decisions and solve problems. In a value-based culture, employees can see the actual connection between work they do and the value proposition IT delivers.

Company culture must enable employees to follow up on value-based objectives

Most profit leaks in IT are not caused by the methodology used, technology chosen, or process followed. They are a product of the culture and values driving wrong behaviors.

For example, a root cause analysis (RCA) program can investigate an incident or outage using the most progressive methods in the industry, but if the culture doesn't allow employees to admit mistakes, companies cannot uncover the real factors causing the defects. More importantly, companies will repeat this cycle over and over versus remediating the problem.

In these cultures, actionable information about the real problems in IT cannot penetrate through an invisible ceiling so that senior leadership understands what the real problems are. Instead, leadership is told what they want to hear, not what they need to know. Further, employees are not rewarded or encouraged to hold peers and leadership accountable for their outcomes.

IT organizations need flexibility to adapt to current circumstances

Rather than running IT like a retail food chain or a factory, IT should operate like a dot-com, using a flexible, tactical, and adaptive delivery methodology to increase scale and quality while reducing cost.

Although automation and managed services can reduce some costs, implementing automation and managed services where they don't belong can make accomplishing the company's objectives harder than it needs to be.

Sustainable growth requires taking a 360-degree look at the IT strategy, including technology, process, scorecards, financials, staffing, and employee/customer engagement. Doing so enables the IT organization to retain the flexibility it needs to adapt and innovate in order to meet users' and customers' needs.

Developing the roadmap requires a consultative mindset

To develop the IT roadmap for projects and services, successful consulting firms approach clients using an integrative negotiation (win-win), where all parties cooperate to achieve maximum benefits while dividing the value. Each makes trade-offs to get the things they value most while giving up less critical factors. Everyone bargains collaboratively and focuses on value, not concessions or financial limitations.

Transitioning to value-based IT isn't always a clear-cut process

When an IT transformation is underway, IT organizations need to remind customers of IT that the journey is not always an A-to-B or straight path with predictable costs and outcomes. When new information becomes available, the IT strategy must adapt in scope, deliverables, costs, and time-lines in the long-term best interests of the users and customers. The ability to adapt is only possible when projects and services are seen through value-based lens and criteria.

IT and customers understand and trust the metrics

In a value-based approach, measurements are established that IT and customers can understand and trust. This ensures accountability for outcomes is transparent to all.

Far too often, IT scorecards results are doctored and do not reflect the true nature of IT services, operations, and projects thereby reducing IT's credibility with customers and IT resources alike. To prevent this, criteria for measurements should be simple and easy to quantify. For example, for project tracking, the matrix could look Table 3-2.

TABLE 3-2   Project Health Criteria

	Green	Yellow	Red
General	On-track	Potential impacts due to project dependencies	Project dependencies preventing project progress
	Progressing as planned	Resource unavailability impacting project	Stakeholder engagement or sign-off preventing project progress
		Stakeholder unavailability impacting project	On hold or cancelled
Schedule	0-10% variance from last baseline	10-15% variance from last baseline	> 15% variance from last baseline
Costs	0-10% variance from last baseline	10-15% variance from last baseline	> 15% variance from last baseline
Risks	No unmanaged risks or issues	Unmitigated, high-probability risks	Unmanaged, high-impact issues
		Unmanaged impacts and/or issues	Status for a single issue Yellow for 3 weeks

When value-based IT organizations create a culture where projects and services accurately report the health without punishment, they can more effectively address underlying factors that are causing the problem — whether those causes are systems, vendors, staffing, skill set gaps, or dependencies with other IT teams and stakeholders.

A balance exists between profit and value

Because IT organizations cannot take their eyes off financial responsibil- ities for operating expenditure budgets (OPEX) and capital expenditure planning, the key is to strike the optimal balance between profit- and value-based approaches. This includes approaching IT challenges with the right mindset to identify desired outcomes first and then work backwards into the profit-based or financial obstacles. This will be explored more later in this chapter and in Part II.

You won't get "cheaper, faster, better," but you can pick any two

"Cheaper, faster, better" leads to IT failures, in part, because these three objectives are in tension with each other. Whether a company is delivering a project or architecting the IT operations and support services model, the Project Management Triangle, shown in Figure 3-1, illustrates how "cheaper, faster, better" are in opposition.

Traditionally, these constraints have been listed as scope (or quality), time, and cost. Because one side of the triangle cannot be changed without affecting the others, the common belief is, "Pick any two."

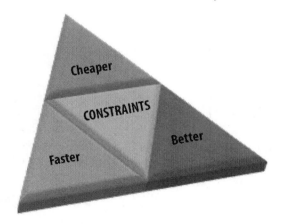

Figure 3-1

The triangle reflects how the three properties are interrelated and how it's not possible to optimize all three because one will always suffer. In other words, the IT organization has three options:

- Design something faster and to a higher standard (better), but then it will not be cheaper.
- Design something faster and cheaper, but it will not be of high quality (better).
- Design something better (higher quality) and cheaper, but not faster.

Introducing the Building Blocks of Value-Based IT

To implement a value-based strategy for an IT organization, focus first on the desired outcomes (value proposition of IT versus cost). Then, work backwards into actions, investments, and required behaviors to achieve these outcomes.

Approaching IT strategy in this way involves a three-step approach:

1. **Balance desired outcomes with the client's needs.** Determine the factors that define the client's improved condition.

2. **Define the activities.** Identify the key activities or actions that must be taken to accomplish the outcomes (goals and objectives).

3. **Align investments with value-driven outcomes and desired behaviors.** This includes IT investments in both physical and human assets.

These steps are the foundation for any IT transformation.

Step 1: Balance desired outcomes with the client's needs.

Today, most metrics to measure IT performance focus on project milestones, costs, burn rates, tickets closed, or system uptime. In a value-based model, qualitative and quantitative measures are tied to clear improvements for clients (users or customers). This ensures IT employees and vendors alike are incentivized to do more than just see IT engagements as a T&M (time and materials) opportunity.

Because value-based measurements can be subjective and other variables will affect outcomes, care must be taken to clearly document the client's needs, past and current state, and future expectations. With this documentation, the IT organization can effectively measure progress and ultimately the client's improved condition.

For example, providing new system functionality or 24/7 system availability does not always improve the client's condition. A finance team's processes remain fairly static over time. The team uses financial systems primarily Monday through Friday and on weekends only at end-of-month close. In this case, system performance and a friendly user interface may be the value proposition, because the recovery time objective (RTO) could be as much as 8 hours before impacting critical business operations.

In contrast, a call center that's open 24/7 would be crippled by a brief outage (1 hour or less), and this outage could result in losing long-time customers. As I explain in more detail in Chapter 5, desired outcomes for the customers of IT can be different for each technical service center.

Whether planning an IT project or an organizational strategy, start by identifying desired outcomes for the clients of that IT service area — that is, setting distinct goals and objectives for the strategy to be measured. In the same way a project has a charter that defines the project scope, value-based IT departments create clarity about who the customer is and what are the types of services they require.

Defining the desired outcomes in simple language is key to developing the measurements that drive the behavior of the IT resources.

Step 2: Define activities or goals to support the desired outcomes

Most likely, IT organizations unknowingly create the problems they are trying to solve because culture, goals, and metrics determine how the IT workforce prioritizes objectives.

For example, a scorecard objective to reduce the total cost of ownership (TCO) may promote an application-centric environment in an effort to control the cost of licensing and the maintenance, hardware, staffing, and skill sets required. In this approach, IT unilaterally makes decisions about what solutions to use, such as ERP, BI, CRM, HRIS, or Web Portals, without fully considering the client's needs. However, does the software promoted provide the key functionality that users or customers need to accomplish their goals and thus can they use the solution to meet all their business needs?

Unfortunately, without the opportunity to buy into the new solution, users and customers are often reluctant to provide the needed support to map business processes, develop use cases, or work through the pain that comes with any software solution adoption. In some cases, employees and business partners then seek IT products and services elsewhere, perhaps dealing directly with vendors for cloud solutions and/or on premise solutions, resulting in new pockets of IT. Then, employees and business partners later engage IT to develop bi-directional interfaces between systems or ask for infrastructure to host the new software applications (often with a short timeline to deliver due to contractual agreements with the software vendor). This is an example of an undesired customer behavior that has consequences for IT.

In contrast, in a value-based approach, the vision and goal might be to ensure that IT solutions support all the features that clients need to accomplish their work. In this case, the objective leads IT to proactively partner with customer to shape the demand for IT services and demonstrates flexibility to fairly assess all solutions to support users' needs. More often than not, this partnership creates trust that positions IT to upsell the benefits of the preferred software applications and prevents clients from introducing new technologies to the landscape. Choosing these types of activities as part of the IT strategy can change IT customers' behavior.

The activities undertaken can change more than just customer outcomes. When architecting an IT strategy — whether a technology roadmap, delivery methodology, or strategic sourcing — organizations must consider the behaviors they want from the IT teams. For example, if teams are expected to adapt to changing circumstances (such as welcoming changing requirements, even late in development, so that the solution is done right the first time), then perhaps Agile and release schedules aren't the way to go. As mentioned in Chapter 2's discussion of Agile, the introduction of sprints and major release cycles can prevent project teams from doing the needed change control for fear of missing a scheduled release. Instead, the teams are rewarded for building solutions quickly and on-time versus in a scalable fashion.

When financial goals are balanced with usability, scalability, and supportability, IT costs become optimal. *Optimal* means that IT costs exactly what is required to bring business strategies to fruition while fostering employee and business partner engagement to achieve maximum productivity. Put simply, a value-based approach ensures IT users and customers are receiving maximum value for dollars spent — not the lowest cost. The question of adopting outsourcing, ITIL, Agile, or other industry best practices is best answered *after* the value proposition of IT is clearly defined versus when determining how to manage the cost of IT.

In value-based IT, organizations do not start with a solution
(cheaper, faster, better) in search of a problem to solve. Instead,
IT seeks to understand the distinct needs of each customer
in order to determine what steps to take that will support the
desired outcomes and needs.

Step 3: Align investments with value-driven outcomes and desired behaviors

The wrong investments may provide some short-term benefits (including higher bonuses and stock options) but often fail to provide real long-term transformation and success for IT. For example, investment decisions motivated by reducing OPEX budgets often fall into this category. Although costs should be minimized whenever possible, achieving lower-cost models alone cannot drive the IT strategy.

When the customers' needs are considered with equal weight as financial targets, then adjustments can be made to IT OPEX budgets and investments to align with the IT value proposition. As we will explore in the IT Business Modeling chapter later in this book, these budgets and investments take into consideration the type of cost structure needed for IT to support the customer needs. Today, IT uses multiple cost structures, and many organizations have a blended approach depending on the service area and services being provided:

- **Profit-driven:** Focuses on minimizing costs using low-cost value propositions, automation, ITIL/ITSM/Agile, and outsourcing.
- **Value-driven:** Focuses on creating a high-value proposition and a high degree of service (often personalized or white-glove service and support).
- **Fixed costs:** Costs remain the same independent of the volume of goods or services produced or received (employees, facilities, software and hardware maintenance/licensing).
- **Variable costs:** Costs can increase and decrease proportionally to the volume of goods and services produced or received (system size and usage, outside and managed services).
- **Economies of scale:** Consolidates services, departments, projects, and environments to reduce the total cost of ownership (sharing technology and human assets).

The investments made and cost structures adopted determine the IT organization's ability to deliver on the IT promise. Equally important is making sure the customers of IT understand the relationship between the costs they are paying and the type service this will provide. For example, a fixed cost structure may not provide white-glove or personalized service. This is why there is a 1:1 mapping between the customer relationship type and the cost structure needed to support that relationship.

To ensure proper alignment, using a value-based framework during the budget planning cycle captures the cost of both physical and human assets required to create scalable solutions to support strategic goals and critical business processes. You find more details about this framework in Chapter 5.

The key is finding the balance between cost-driven and value-driven cost structures mindful that creating and delivering value to the client while maintaining customer relationships will always incur more costs than expected. The value proposition of IT is measured by the benefits provided to the customers, not the cost savings found.

Chapter Summary

For a company to shift its thinking away from profit-based IT and toward value-based IT, the organization needs to understand the value-based mindset. The primary difference between the two models comes down to focus and philosophy:

- Profit-based focuses on the cost of IT services, operations, and initiatives.
- Value-based focuses on usability, adoption, scalability, and supportability.

Moreover, a value-based mindset supports the following:

- Gives employees a clear purpose of what they are here to do.
- Enables the organization or employees to admit mistakes in order to continue moving toward the desired outcomes or purpose.
- Allows for flexibility to meet immediate needs or circumstances.
- Encourages a consultative mindset between IT and its users or customers.
- Acknowledges that the steps and transition process may not always be clear or straightforward as knowledge is gathered and new information comes to light.
- Creates transparency by defining metrics that both IT and customers alike can trust.

- Balances profit and value and acknowledges that the IT organization can't realistically accomplish "cheaper, faster, better," because these three objectives are in conflict with each other. However, accomplishing two of these is realistic.

In a value-based approach, you don't start with a budget in mind and figure what you can afford to do that year. Instead, desired outcomes and behaviors are defined and actions are mapped. Only then is the IT organization ready to explore how to pay to achieve the goals or renegotiate the IT value proposition with the customer and senior leadership.

The next chapter focuses on a value-based case study illustrating how one company applied the concepts outlined in this chapter to its specific circumstances.

While the value-based model outlined in this chapter lays the foundational layer for the IT transformation, the Six Protocols, which I cover in Part II, provide the common language, rules, and processes that enable companies to apply the value-based principles. The Six Protocols accomplish the following:

- Better translate strategic goals and critical business processes into scalable IT solutions.

- Drive higher accountability for IT to reduce defects, prevent rework, and improve quality.

- Develop sourcing strategies to continuously improve vendor outcomes and reduce cost.

- Create scale, increase throughput, and accelerate speed to market for solutions.

CHAPTER 4

AN ERP CASE STUDY FOR VALUE-BASED IT

Even when organizational strategies appear profit-driven, IT departments and teams can champion a value-based culture. The case study in this chapter shows how a $10 billion dollar distribution business achieved value-based outcomes in an organization with a profit-based mindset.

In this case study, the SAP Projects and Operations organization had been supporting the business unit on a dedicated instance of SAP for five years. Two years earlier, the business unit had completed a merger and acquisition that doubled its revenue as well as users and order volumes. Further, system upgrades were behind six enhancement packs, hardware was at end of life and undersized, RDBMS support was on extended maintenance at a premium cost, and the A2A/B2B technology was over 5 years old.

In light of system health, or lack thereof, at the enterprise IT level, the desired outcomes were mapped (see Step 1 in Chapter 3) and four objectives identified for the SAP department. Three were aligned with the value proposition and one with a profit-based objective:

- **Scale:** Scale the SAP expertise and processes to execute projects to support business growth.
- **Quality:** Base the delivery model on best practices, standards, and governance to reduce defects, drive efficiency, and manage risks.
- **Operational Excellence:** Provide 99.9 percent system availability and deliver on project commitments with no business disruption (white glove service).
- **Cost:** Keep IT budgets flat year over year (or reduce costs).

Creating Scale

To accomplish the objectives (or outcomes), the IT leadership explored the needed activities and investments to drive desired behaviors. However, there wasn't a consensus on what activities were needed or behaviors desired. Senior leadership advocated collecting more operational metrics on incident tickets and monitoring how people spent their time, including asking employees to perform additional administrative timekeeping details. The enterprise IT leadership believed that collecting more data points and scripting what everyone was doing (more oversight) would incentivize employees to be more productive. Further, enterprise IT leadership believed this data could be used to engage managed services to outsource IT services and support and thus reduce costs.

The SAP Applications Director chose a different set of activities and investments: piloting a proof-of-concept for outsourcing in two areas to give a vendor a chance to demonstrate the value proposition the vendor could bring. This proof-of-concept included the following:

- A six-month pilot using a managed services vendor for quality control (testing services) that could be easily scripted in test plans and transitioned to offshore.

- A six-month pilot using a managed services vendor for support and project work with a small footprint (a headcount of one to five resources) to ensure the managed services provider had both the competency and ability to scale resources.

The quality control managed services vendor was able to quickly take over testing and developed a strategy to build a Test Center of Excellence (TCoE), including regression libraries, a document management system, and a knowledge base for critical business processes. In addition, the vendor brought new levels of innovation around testing, including tools at no cost to the organization. The vendor reduced defects and improved outcomes for day-to-day changes as well as large projects at half the cost of full-time employees and one-fourth the cost of professional services resources. Furthermore, by establishing regression libraries for order to cash, procure to pay, financials, and so on, the vendor streamlined other areas like upgrade remediation testing, disaster recovery exercises verification, and 21 CFR Part 11 FDA validation. Using managed services ultimately freed up more experienced analysts and developers to focus on key projects and complex problem tickets, which enabled the SAP team to scale (triple its throughput in project hours over a 12-month period)

However, the support and projects pilot to create scale and reduce costs using a managed services vendor was not as successful. Resources were thoroughly interviewed to ensure they brought the right expertise for their functional area and quickly picked up the systems and local processes. However, to support the desired outcome of white-glove service, more on-site than off-shore resources were required, reducing the cost savings from the blended off-shore model. In the end, managed services did not provide the needed scale in projects and support for several reasons:

- Locking into a single vendor limited the talent pool and skill sets available (such as industry knowledge for life sciences).
- The on-site rate cards were not more competitive than those in the Vendor Management System (VMS) for hiring contingent labor.
- When resources needed to be co-located in one of four physical sites, this limited the talent pool even further and caused additional travel and relocation expenses.
- Finding qualified candidates for open requisitions took months. In contrast, using a VMS, requisitions were posted and filled within two to four weeks on average. The VMS also made it easier to find candidates local to one of the four locations.

Additionally, unlike the quality control example, the managed service vendor did not introduce any new levels of innovation for support or make recommendations on improving service levels.

Before committing to a long-term strategy and master service agreement (MSA) with any vendor, pilot the program to verify the trusted key partner has competence, can scale quickly, and can sustain or improve existing service levels. For projects specifically, remember, when you can control the competency of the resources, you can predict the outcomes.

Delivering Quality and Operational Excellence

Next, the IT team collaborated internally across verticals (development, functional, QA and project management) to identify what activities and investments would be needed to drive operational excellence in light of the budget constraints and system health.

The SAP team started by establishing better controls for the increasing number of system changes (or transports) moving through the fragile SAP environment. The first goal was to prevent outages versus responding more quickly when outages occur.

To improve IT governance, change-management processes were reviewed to ensure that code, data, configuration, and objects were being migrated correctly and tracked accurately from system to system, thereby ensuring that changes to a production environment were introduced in a coordinated manner. This reduced the possibility that unnecessary changes resulted in system conflicts or defects. The goal was to reduce disruptions to services and back-out activities to ensure cost-effective use of key resources involved in implementing changes.

To further mitigate risks and lower costs of ownership, the IT team invested in implementing change-control management software. This software integrated workflow with email alerts and reminders of work pending, which helped automate this critical activity and streamline operations. The tool embedded all required documentation (attachments) or document references (links), fulfilling audit and compliance enforcement of predetermined processes, segregation of duties, electronic signatures, and regulatory processes (SOX, FDA CFR Part 11, and so on).

Second, the team explored what actions and investments were needed to address the increasing cost of support for the growing number of SAP users and B2B accounts (external customers). In other words, the team needed to figure out how to handle more work while managing costs. To solve this, the more seasoned and expensive contractors were mapped from working support tickets to billable projects to recoup their costs in the project re-class financial process. Lower-cost contractors were hired and trained for routine or day-to-day operations. To facilitate knowledge transfer and provide oversight, internal full-time employees were paired up with the new lower-cost contractors. By using a blend of full-time employees and lower-cost contractors, over a period of time, the average cost per hour reduced 19 percent ($26 per hour) generating $52,000 savings for every 2,000 hours of support. Note that all the resources were on-shore and fully integrated into the IT delivery organization.

As shown in Figure 4-1, the average cost for contingent labor in support was $129 per hour in Q1 FY13. By Q2 FY14, the average cost was $103 per hour. This was a $26 dollar per hour reduction in operating costs.

Figure 4-1 Support —Average Contractor Rates

Keep in mind, the value-based outcome was not to get services at the cheapest price, but rather to create scale that supported operations while keeping budgets flat. As an added benefit, more full-time employees were able to work on projects after lower-cost contractors gained competency in the systems. This model motivated and helped retain talented employees and increased productivity by giving internal employees growth opportunities in their fields of expertise.

Moving full-time employees to project work also helped keep budgets flat, because full-time employees don't bill time and materials, yet their costs can be recouped from capital budgets (billed out higher than their fully burdened costs). Finally, when given stretch goals and new opportunities, FTEs often work longer hours tirelessly to ensure the success of the project at no additional cost to the project.

While solving the problem of creating scale and keeping budgets flat, the SAP team also found new ways drive operational efficiencies without impacting service levels. The solution included using managed services for testing at lower costs (as noted earlier) and increasing the allocation model for billing out full-time employees to fund the needed staffing levels to transform the delivery model. To cover the costs of using contractors for support, the billing rate for full-time employees was increased from $76 to $89 per hour on projects, which was still significantly lower than contingent labor for the same skill sets. The key is leveraging internal employees already in the OPEX budget for project work and billing their time out to cost centers or a project WBS code. This generates income for the IT cost center above the original plan.

As a result, costs for projects and support decreased, and project delivery teams tripled capacity over one year, meeting the peak demand. Both contractors and full-time employees alike took on additional project work (evenly) versus scaling only with contractor resources. I should note that the project work didn't use dedicated scrum teams, and all full-time employees served as shared resources for both projects and operations during this period. Instead, each week, at a resource and capacity planning meeting, resource managers decided how to assign work.

Keeping IT Budgets Flat

Because the scorecard objective was to keep IT costs flat while driving operational efficiencies, creating scale was not possible by hiring more seasoned (expensive) consultants for projects to ensure project success.

The SAP team also faced another challenge that the defined outcomes didn't consider: In the early years of the ERP implementation and during the merger and acquisition, the SAP department could always redirect some of its leftover capital and expense budget to help cover growing costs without increasing IT OPEX budgets. However, after the new ERP implementation and merger and acquisition were complete, these funds dried up, leaving the business unit and IT feeling the squeeze to control costs and to increase EBIT. This is the typical time when companies explore "cheaper, faster, better" solutions.

What activities and investments were made? To solve this, three things were changed:

- The entire organization was considered one IT delivery team (projects and support). Resources could move seamlessly between roles. The IT delivery team did not map to separate scrum teams or support teams (verticals).

- Managed services was used for testing services. This cut testing costs between 50-75 percent, freeing up resources and dollars to be used for other more critical needs.

- The delivery model was flipped so that internal employees filled key roles on projects, and less expensive and less experienced contractors backfilled the employees' routine enhancements and support activities.

  - As mentioned earlier, to help fund using contigent labor to backfill full-time employees, the allocation model changed full-time employees' billing rate from $76 per hour to $89 per hour.
  - Discussions took place with business partners, explaining the new full-time employee rate was still 32 percent lower than the average professional services rate, and thus enabled the company to save money on labor overall.

Not only did these measures reduce total cost for delivery of IT solutions, the measures gave internal employees meaningful work on larger projects and a chance to build new skills, and strengthened client relationships. As the compentecy of the internal SAP team members grew, rolling off long-term, higher-priced contractors —who, in the past, business partners and IT alike were afraid of letting go — became easier. After internal employees gained exposure to projects, business partners began trusting these resources to backfill the higher-paid consultants. In addition, this positioned IT to negotiate better rate cards for all new contractors, because internal team members were able to play the technical lead roles on projects. In some cases, old agreements (rate cards) at much higher rates were lowered or the resources were rolled off and replaced with lower-cost contractors.

The outcomes included creating more scale by increasing the use of full-time employees on projects versus just adding more outside services for projects. With contingent labor costing an average rate of $150 per hour or more for projects, shifting this work to full-time employees (whose average fully burdened costs was less than $78 an hour), the company saved money. Further, as depicted in Figure 4-2, the outcomes included tripling the project hours over a one-year period, creating the needed scale while driving cost savings for the business.

Figure 4-2 Project Hours Over Six Quarters

Although project work and demand for additional resources increased, this model allowed new contractors to be hired at lower rates because the IT department had the in-house expertise to lead projects and design solutions. As shown in Figure 4-3, during an 18-month period, the hourly rate for professional services dropped over 16 percent ($25 per hour). This meant for every 2,000 hours of project work, the company was spending $50,000 less when using contractors on IT projects.

Figure 4-3 Project—Average Contractor Rates

One might argue that these savings aren't sustainable over an extended period of time without adopting more outsourcing or methodologies like ITIL, ITSM, or Agile. According to the conventional wisdom in the industry, IT costs always continue to climb with the increasing revenues, order volumes, users, and services offered. However, in this SAP case study, the team created scale, kept IT costs flat, and sustained the same levels in service (the system availability had 99.85 percent uptime) over a five-year period despite over doubling in size.

The outcome is easily quantified with one indisputable value-based metric: growth in revenue compared to IT costs year over year. As noted in Figure 4-4, revenues more than doubled but the budgets remained flat over the five-year period.

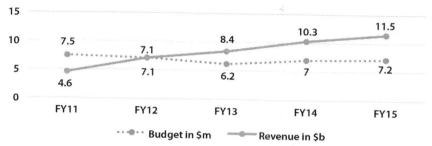

Figure 4-4 *Revenue Growth versus IT Bduget*

Chapter Summary

The company in this case study had two schools of thought on how to accomplish the FY14 goals. In the profit-based approach, enterprise IT leadership advocated the following:

- Restructuring the organization into support and project verticals
- Creating dedicated teams (verticals for support and projects)
- Monitoring the activities of support employees so IT could develop metrics for an RFP to outsource services

The proposed strategy would have replace seasoned analysts and developers with the lower-paid off-shore resources in the hope that, after one or two years, the vendor would build competency in the life sciences industry and the company's SAP environment.

In contrast, the SAP Applications Director chose a value-based approach to drive all decision making around staffing, technology, and process, including piloting a Test Center of Excellence for testing and outsourcing projects and support. The SAP department kept the focus on the outcomes needed to bring the business strategies to fruition, not the OPEX budgets and savings. To do this, the workforce (both SAP users and IT resources) were included in developing the roadmap and decision-making process, thereby creating more clarity and better alignment around top priorities and objectives.

To ensure transparency, ongoing communication channels were established:

- Quarterly SAP applications all hands meeting
- Monthly governance council meetings with key departments
- Monthly contractor checkpoint meeting
- Monthly cost center managers financial review
- Bimonthly SAP shared services review
- Bimonthly SAP operations review
- Bimonthly SAP project review
- Cyclic (weekly or every two weeks) one-on-one meetings with managers
- Weekly capacity planning and prioritization meeting
- Weekly staff meetings

The value-based approach did not focus on short-term budget limitations and financial obstacles. Instead, the strategy focused on desired outcomes and worked backwards to deal with financials, territorial, or political challenges.

This case study illustrates how a value-based culture enabled IT to increase scale without increasing cost. More importantly, the value-based model built trust that the IT department is constantly driving increased value for the money it spends. Stakeholders also learned to trust the IT team to execute on its promises with precision and predictability.

At the end of the day, whether IT is considering is a $50K enhancement or a $3 million project, clients are not looking for the lowest-cost solution. They are looking for the expected value for IT dollars spent.

This case study illustrates how IT teams can deliver on commitments while reducing costs. They need not set the bar lower by adopting a fail-forward-fast strategy or accepting project failure rates of 20-28 percent as the norm. Further, IT doesn't require external experts to develop the roadmap. The two factors that enabled this IT success are the value-based strategy and organizational health.

IMPLEMENTING VALUE-BASED IT: THE FIRST FIVE PROTOCOLS FOR MANAGING IT TRANSFORMATION

CHAPTER 5

FIRST PROTOCOL:
IT BUSINESS MODELING

Creating an IT organization that works in harmony within IT and with clients requires focus on five separate but tightly integrated areas, as shown in Figure 5-1. Unfortunately, companies tend to focus on only one or two protocols at any given time, never fully aligning them all for optimal results. When a company considers all the protocols in concert, teams are more committed to improving the client's condition, productivity is higher, costs are optimal, and the stage is set for industry-changing innovation from the IT population that drives competitive advantage.

Figure 5-1

What does it mean to consider all the protocols in concert? Consider this example. An organization can have solid methodology for project delivery or operations, focus on customers in order to the provide value proposition promised, and manage the IT brand (business partner engagement) thoughtfully. However, the same organization can choose to rely too heavily on outside services, not hire and staff key positions internally, and neglect to provide controls for oversight of vendors. In this situation, IT still won't be able to deliver on commitments. Therefore, when shaping the Enterprise IT strategy, all protocols and interdependencies must be considered.

This chapter focuses on the First Protocol, IT Business Modeling (ITBM). In this protocol, IT leadership defines desired outcomes and expectations for the IT organization. Careful analysis ensures that teams aren't pursuing the wrong goals and that the IT strategy aligns with what customers really want and need. That is, IT's value proposition is clear to both IT and customers.

**IT Business Modeling ensures the puzzle pieces for
IT fit together.**

Introducing Value-Based IT Business Modeling

Profit-driven organizations prefer a top-down approach to modeling IT strategy by standardizing all processes to reduce cost. In some cases, IT organizations attempt to standardize processes by turning over design, control, and accountability of the strategy to an outside vendor.

A value-based organization uses ITBM to improve IT's value to the customer by identifying and providing distinct IT services that cater to clients' needs. Value-based ITBM ensures the IT strategy is locally owned, relevant, and understandable to all while addressing the challenges and complexity of the IT enterprise. Through ITBM, companies approach their strategy with the mindset that IT has to sell its business model to investors and also win or retain client business to survive.

Creating a complete planning cycle

Today, in most companies, discussions on strategy, the IT roadmap, goals, objectives, rewards, and budgets happen at different times of the year. However, ITBM consolidates these discussions into one complete planning cycle, including defining measurements before the new fiscal year begins. Fixed, semi-variable, employee, and asset costs for budget planning happen in conjunction with developing the technology roadmap, developing goals, assessing staffing needs, and planning for performance management.

Additionally, each year, the business model is reevaluated to determine what has changed, including a thorough review of the following areas:

- What customers and needs have been added or removed?
- Are key physical or human resources adequate for the expected growth in demand?

- What new partnerships are needed to manage costs or improve outcomes?
- How will changes in customer's needs, new services, and key partnerships be translated into goals, objectives, and rewards for employees?
- How will IT measure the success, and are the measurements trusted?

Following the basic ITBM framework

For the ITBM discussion, standard business modeling practices are adapted into a common IT framework shared across the IT ecosystem. You use the same framework whether you're modeling infrastructure services (networks, databases, and so on), ERP services (sales, distribution, financials, and so on), or external customer-facing services (Web portal, customer care). The following steps outline the universal framework for value-based ITBM:

1. Understanding IT users and business partners (customers)
2. Managing customer relationships (engagement)
3. Defining IT's value proposition
4. Identifying the physical and intellectual resources needed to deliver the desired outcomes
5. Defining measurements (scorecards)
6. Establishing IT partners relationships (internal and external)
7. Identifying IT revenue streams (budgets) and managing costs
8. Developing a cost structure

Each step in this framework is explained in more detail later in this chapter.

Approaching IT strategy from the bottom up

Industry data on failed IT projects and outsourcing brings into question the paradigm of making large transformational changes across the IT enterprise to drive savings or increase scale. In fact, letting the enterprise dictate one common strategy for each technical service center (TSC) is like shooting an arrow at night and then waiting until sunrise to see if you hit the target.

Real, sustainable savings occurs through a number of small improvements in each area of the enterprise. Here's an overview of how the bottom-up ITBM process works:

1. Start at the lowest level (technical service center). First, each team documents all assessments and expected outcomes locally.

2. Roll up to the department level. Each TSC shares the results of its assessments, findings, and outcomes with other departments to find economies of scale.

3. Integrate TSC- and department-level findings at the enterprise level, where company leadership can identify all partnerships required to drive economies of scale (for both physical and human assets).

ITBM analysis always begins from the customer's perspective at the level of the technical service center. This approach enables teams to set short-term goals that move the dial on improving IT services and reducing costs while ensuring teams have the autonomy needed to make tactical decisions.

To ensure alignment across the enterprise and business, ITBM is performed during the budgeting cycle, inclusive of all factors (company goals, IT roadmap, scorecards, and performance management objectives). A week or more should be set aside annually to facilitate workshops at each level. Then TSCs, departments, and enterprise IT can align for optimum outcomes.

If performing ITBM for the first time, companies may develop a beta or pilot program by prototyping the ITBM process with a couple technical service centers in one department. The goal is to explore, discover, and ultimately design a simple, repeatable process that all teams and departments can adapt. After the pilot TSCs define the process, then the other service areas and departments can try the process until the company identifies a common set of practices for training managers and senior leaders across the organization.

Following the Universal Framework for Value-Based IT Business Modeling

As mentioned earlier in this chapter, value-based ITBM has a universal framework that companies can follow as they evaluate their IT strategy at each level of the business, starting at the bottom, or TSC, level. The following sections explore how companies can implement each part of this framework successfully.

Understanding the customer's distinct needs

IT serves customers with different and distinct needs: IT customers include external companies and internal departments who use IT services.

Customers can also be other IT departments. In all cases, the Technical Service Center needs to define the services required.

To understand the distinct needs of each customer, first ask, "For whom am I creating value?" As I explain earlier, each customer of IT might have unique needs. Financial and marketing teams rely heavily on analytics, whereas a distribution division needs its transaction system and processes streamlined to decrease costs and increase throughput.

To ensure IT services are aligned with each customer's needs, catalog who exactly the TSC customer is by answering the following questions:

- **What service areas do these customers belong to?** Your answers might include different departments (such as distribution, marketing, and human resources) or even another TSC.
- **What type of relationship is required to serve this customer?** By relationship type, I mean automation or human interaction. Different groups might require a combination of both.
- **What are each customer's success factors and goals?**
- **What does each customer need from IT to ensure their competitive advantage?**

Identifying the customer base and type ensures that IT strategy considers the business's diversified needs. Distinct services may fall into various categories, ranging from a niche software to support, such as a customer relationship management tool like Salesforce.com, to a business intelligence tool like Tableau. Some customers have more complex and diversified needs, such as an entire ERP environment that supports order-to-cash, procure-to-pay, and financials. In some cases, the customer is actually another technical service center (IT team).

The key is to create a strong understanding of each customer's needs and then design the approach for each customer segment to improve that customer's condition in a measurable way.

Here are a few examples of how you might measure whether IT is meeting a customer's needs:

- Distribution operations are measured on packages shipped and orders filled.
- Credit and collections are measured on Days Sales Outstanding (DSO).
- Financial planning and analysis (FP&A) is concerned with the number of days it takes to perform a month-end-close.

The technical service center needs to understand these variations and account for the unique needs across segments of its internal customers.

Even within the ERP order-to-cash module, the value proposition and service levels may vary for the Web portal, call centers, and EDI order channels — each requiring a different offering and unique service levels:

- Web portals might focus on response times, whereas EDI can be more forgiving with performance and time needed to transmit documents.

- Call centers might need additional security and flexibility to address customer services (such as adding credit cards) not possible through just any order channel.

As part of the ITBM process, the TSCs capture the service level agreements (SLAs) for each customer segment they support in order to develop a meaningful way to measure the value proposition that IT delivers to the client. This is step one in defining the ITBM.

Managing and maintaining customer relationships

In a typical business modeling approach, customers are categorized into generic relationship types to ensure the success of the business. In IT, the TSCs also need to identify the type of relationship required for each customer segment. The following list outlines some common relationship types shared across the IT industry. Each customer of IT could map into one or more of the following categories:

- **Dedicated support:** White-glove personal assistance, where select resources are assigned to handle all needs for the client.

- **Personal assistance:** The clients can count on human interaction for their needs. They can call, email, IM, text, or in some cases, have direct physical access to IT personnel for support.

- **Self-service:** The organization provides tools enabling IT customers to serve themselves easily and effectively. This might be to reset a password for security, request additional system access, or to submit a service catalog request to order products and services (such as Web conferencing, PCs, and so on).

- **Business request:** This may include portfolio management solutions for submitting a project request as well as an incident or change-request ticket. The IT request triggers workflow, and IT assistance is provided internally or by a vendor in accordance with service levels established for the severity and priority of the request.

- **911 request:** This skirts all predefined processes, and IT executes on the time-sensitive request outside of prescribed procedures and processes.

For the customers in each segment, each TSC clarifies the approach, justification, and cost if a customer requests a premium service. TSCs and departments work with customers to leverage automation where it makes sense, such as security and service catalog activities. Here are few examples of how different customers who might need dedicated support or personal assistance:

- The legal department, which deals with time-sensitive requests for adjudication (like response to a subpoena), may require personal assistance.
- Distribution centers measured on orders filled and packages shipped cannot afford delays associated with an automated incident service request process and thus expect dedicated support.
- The FP&A team may require personal assistance only at month-end, quarter-end, or year-end close when the team cannot afford to miss deadlines without significant financial consequences.

When this exercise is performed correctly, corresponding allocation models (costs) can be adjusted to account for customers' distinct needs.

Defining IT's value proposition

Customer value proposition (CVP) is the total benefit promised to a customer in return for an associated payment. In IT, value propositions are the products and services that create value for the customer. Typically, the CVP concept targets potential customers rather than internal system users or business partners.

To build a successful ITBM, IT leadership needs to clearly define IT's value proposition. The value proposition statement must explain how IT products and/or services create value and solve the customers' business problems better than others who could compete for the same business. This competitive mindset shifts the focus from profit-driven goals of reducing costs to increasing customer satisfaction.

In a typical CVP exercise for IT, TSCs list all the benefits that they believe they deliver. Moreover, the TSC differentiates one product or service from another relative to the needs of each customer.

To differentiate products and services effectively, the TSC engages its customers to gain a detailed understanding of their requirements and preferences. For example, a TSC for business intelligence must document the unique reporting needs of finance, marketing, legal, distribution centers, and so on. The CVP then becomes an aggregate of all clients' needs and represents a complete bundle of products and services required to satisfy the TSC's customer base.

To clarify the level detail needed in a CVP, here are a few examples:

- Implementing a financial supply chain model is not a value proposition. However, configuring a financial supply chain model to provide workflow and alerts to reduce Days Sales Outstanding (DSO) is a value proposition.
- Installing an appliance like HANA (High-Performance Analytic Appliance) is not a value proposition. Instead, a value proposition is improving performance and response times for high transaction rates and complex query processing to support critical business.

The CVP process reveals how IT can or does provide value to each customer. Generally speaking, a CVP typically reveals results such as the following:

- Business units performing heavy analytics (such as marketing or Six Sigma) may require new software and technology to keep pace with market innovations to gain competitive advantage.
- A business intelligence offering for some users may need to homogenously integrate across multiple enterprise data warehouses (EDWs) or with external industry data.
- FP&A users typically have fairly static demands for services, but value is defined as the confidence that all reports tie back to the system of record. Also, for this group, it's important to ensure all reports perform during peak demand periods, such as month-end close.
- Distribution center business partners may need to customize standard ERP functionality to adapt software technologies for internal processes that optimize operations, streamline pick/pack/ship activities, and reduce costs.

All TSCs share one common characteristic: They exist to serve a customer. Developing the TSC's value proposition goes hand-in-hand with understanding the distinct needs, service levels, and customer relationship types for each segment that the TSC serves.

Whether developing the value proposition for an established customer or a new offering, the approach is the same:

1. Develop a profile for each customer segment.
2. Understand what customers are trying to accomplish or the work they are doing (day in the life of their job).

3. Define customers' main challenges (pain points). What are the problems, obstacles, and risks associated with their business?

4. Identify the opportunities (gains) to improve the customer's condition. What are the outcomes the customer wishes to achieve or what improvements need to be driven?

5. Finally, use this information to develop the customer value proposition (CVP).

Identifying the IT resources needed to deliver

After a TSC understands its customer relationship type and value proposition, each TSC determines the resources needed to deliver on commitments. These resources include the physical, intellectual, human, and financial resources required to support day-to-day operations, delivery of projects, and IT services.

These resources can be internal or acquired from outside services. Often, the enterprise determines what physical assets (like facilities, systems, networks, and other related infrastructure) IT has, and the TSC understands it must work within the constraints of those assets.

However, the TSC may have the flexibility to select some software and hardware and have input into the intellectual and human resources needed to make the business model work.

The following sections take a closer look at each type of resource the TSC needs to consider as part of ITBM.

Physical assets

When IT resources (physical and human) are identified during the budget-planning cycle, new capital and/or expense budget is added to the plan for the next fiscal year. This includes all considerations like relocating a team that has outgrown its space or colocating teams to increase work effectiveness when communication and interaction are a crucial part of the work process.

As mentioned earlier, physical assets include facilities, systems, networks, and other related infrastructure. As the TSC determines what physical assets it needs, the CVP is a helpful guide. For example, if distribution centers need to receive alerts about critical business system errors to improve service levels, then the TSC may consider require real-time application performance monitoring software. To provide this service to a distribution center, TSCs may earmark new capital for assets (software or hardware). If the CVP is to reduce costs or allocations back to the business for IT services, the TSC may deploy automation or a self-service model to lower long-term costs.

Intellectual assets

Intellectual assets include IT partnerships with vendors or industry services required for TSCs to fulfill their promises to clients. Intellectual assets might include master service agreements with companies such as IBM, Oracle, SAP, PeopleSoft, or perhaps third-party vendors like Paymetric and SEE-BURGER. Depending on the industry, external databases like First Databank, Medi-Span, or other regulatory data may be integrated into the environment to support the business processes.

After determining the relationship type and value proposition, each TSC decides what internal competencies are required, and whether an outside vendor or more seasoned internal employees are required to deliver the services needed. For example, specialized knowledge for an ERP module like CRM may require partnering with a vendor or acquiring this distinct skill set in-house.

Finally, the ITBM considers what incremental temporary assets are required to improve the client's condition. These assets may include more user training or developing better documentation to reduce incidents and costs.

Human assets

Each TSC determines how many employees and what skill levels are required to achieve its goals. Then the TSC submits staffing projections, including discretionary spending (for expenses like professional services or adding staff). Discretionary spending enables teams to grow and shrink within the limits of the existing budget.

However, the department and enterprise must ensure the budget sets aside money to address an unexpected or emergency spike in demand for IT services. When a workforce-management tool captures project and support hours throughout the year, discretionary spending can be forecasted based on past history. When no historical data exists, TCSs should budget a contingency fund to prepare for unexpected demands or emergencies.

Financial assets

After the TSC knows what assets it needs, the TSC can calculate how much delivering on its IT promise will cost.

Unfortunately, companies that use a top-down approach require departments and the TSCs to agree to financial targets and constraints imposed without input. Often these budgets fall short, sacrificing long-term cost-saving opportunities, such as contractor conversions, system refreshes and upgrades, or implementing a new technology or capability. These financial decisions have a ripple effect, preventing teams from moving the dial in improvement areas that lower IT costs over the long term.

By approaching the budgeting exercise using the ITBM process, the true cost needed to successfully provide the service offering can be measured. The enterprise can choose whether to provide the desired value proposition by making the needed investments and communicate proactively with clients.

Defining scorecard metrics

In the profit-based model, a financial framework, such as ROI or the annual budget, determines strategic goals and tactical objectives. In a value-based framework, quality, customer satisfaction, business processes to improve, and IT resources are the focus. The key is striking the balance between these two models because managing to only one is suboptimal.

Using a balanced scorecard puts strategy at the center of the planning process, creating strategic focus and alignment, which in turn, enables organizations to translate strategy into action. The balanced scorecard approach ensures TSCs and IT departments build scorecards that managers can use to track staff activities and monitor the consequences arising from these activities.

Here's an overview of the elements that create a successful balanced scorecard:

- Each team establishes its own balanced scorecards. That is, the TSC chooses what data to measure and sets the value of expected outcomes.
- A balanced scorecard tracks data related to customer goals, financial targets, employee engagement, and the technology roadmap.
- Scorecard data needs to be easy to quantify. This enables the TSC manager to monitor performance and take corrective actions quickly to change course.

Developing a scorecard that's easy to quantify means choosing measurements that employees and stakeholders can understand and trust. Here are a few issues and considerations common to many TSCs:

- As depicted in the earlier case study, the cost of IT and throughput in hours are easily quantified.
- Measurements such as on-time and on-budget have variables and constraints often outside the control of the team.

- Measuring the time to respond to customer incidents can be quantified with workflow whereas time to close a ticket can depend on outside factors not always in the control of the technical service center.

Remember, the goals and objectives drive employees' behavior, and choose goals and objectives that ultimately improve the efficiency of IT and business operations.

To ensure clarity and alignment across the team, the TSC manager and teams collaborate to catalog all the opportunities for the year. Then, these opportunities are weighted and prioritized. The TSC manager and team agree to the top 8-12 priorities, and these scorecard objectives are tracked and included in the performance-management process.

Ideally, all team members contribute to architecting the scorecard. Although the department provides the defining objectives and qualitative components of the organizational goals, the TSC defines the operational-level objectives and sets the priorities that all team members share. To ensure success, the priorities must be communicated to customers and IT partners (shared services, other TSCs, vendors, and so on) to ensure alignment, including what role they will play in achieving these objectives.

Think of the scorecard as providing a rallying cry around key priorities that everyone in the TSC supports. The scorecard provides data that enables teams, departments, and divisions to work together in order to solve a common goal.

By enabling employees to work together, the scorecard prevents barriers that waste resource time, reduce productivity, and put outcomes at risk. Scorecards eliminate obstacles that derail organizations by providing the context and clarity employees need to collaborate, thereby reducing stress, removing distractions, and minimizing frustration and disengagement.

Using ITBM, the enterprise provides the framework (organization's vision and strategy) that departments and TSCs use to create their operational scorecards. Then teams translate this vision into operational goals and objectives to tactically address the problems. Figure 5-2 is an example of enterprise-level IT objectives that could be cascaded to IT departments and the teams to develop their operational objectives.

Scale
•Scale the IT resources and processes to execute on projects that support business growth

Operational Excellence
•Deliver on all commitments with no business disruption (provide white glove service)

Quality
•Base the delivery model on best practices and governance to drive efficiency / manage risks

Cost
•Keep IT budgets flat year over year

Retain talent
•Create meaningful jobs and career opportunities for growth

Figure 5-2

Using these defining objectives as a guide, the TSC can catalog what they need to do during the year to support enterprise and department goals. Two or three goals are chosen that support the defining objectives and tracked each quarter on the local scorecard (depending on the skill sets needed, sense of urgency, predecessor activities required, and costs/budgets). The scorecard is published to the team and IT partners.

Table 5-1 provides an example of a TSC's operational scorecard that supports the enterprise objectives outlined in Figure 5-2.

TABLE 5-1 Example Department and TSC Scorecard

Strategic Objective	Strategic Measure
Streamline and mature SDLC processes.	In Q1, develop and deliver SOPs and training.
Streamline workforce, portfolio, project, and demand planning.	In Q1, define and design requirements. In Q2, configure and roll out PPM tool.
Establish test automation and Test Center of Excellence (TCoE) and assess outsourcing options.	In Q1, define and design roadmap for TCoE. In Q2, sign MSA with managed services partner.
Create governance to reduce defects and increase accountability.	By end of Q2, develop framework, workflow, and SOPs for program roll out.
Perform an incident management process assessment that reduces incidents/tickets.	In Q2, prepare assessment by reviewing RCAs, processes, and operation metrics.
Perform technology risk assessment.	In Q4, complete a needs assessment and develop an upgrade plan and technology roadmap.
Develop IT roadmap for upgrades, new modules, and capabilities.	In Q4, define the requirements and scope. Then prepare RFP specification and select a proposal.
Provide business analysis training and certification.	By end of Q4, identify, customize, and deliver business analysis training.

At the department and enterprise levels, individual TSC operational score-cards are cross-referenced to discover economies of scale for infrastructure assets (hardware/software), human assets, or IT partnerships (internal/external) to increase speed to market or reduce cost. Sharing scorecards also enables teams to innovate or identify best practices that all TSCs can share.

One final note: IT activities for scorecards should not be confused with employee individual performance objectives, because not all employees will work on specific scorecard objectives. Unfortunately, employees often don't understand the relationship between their assigned tasks, their individual performance objectives, and department scorecards. Worse, when individual performance objectives mimic enterprise or department goals (like creating scale, completing tasks on-time/on-budget, or increasing quality), these individual objectives provide very little clarity for the employee.

Developing the scorecard during ITBM process with detailed objectives makes it easier to translate scorecard objectives into performance objectives for individual employees. When managers can develop each employee's goals, objectives, and rewards in a way that aligns with commitments made but speaks in employee-specific language, the scorecards are more likely to drive the desired outcomes across the IT department.

To ensure accountability, the expected outcomes and actual outcomes are published throughout the year. This way, each TSC understands how they succeeded or failed to deliver on their commitments.

Establishing IT partner relationships

Partner relationships include all alliances required to attain the assets that optimize the business model, reduce risks, and deliver IT's value proposition. These relationships include those you have with vendors, suppliers, internal technical service centers, and business partners.

In ITBM, each TSC defines and catalogs its partnerships required for its mission by answering the following questions:

- Who are the TSCs' IT partners today?
- What new IT partners are required to support the scorecard objectives?
- What do we need from these partners?
- What resources can the partners provide (intellectual, physical, human, or financial)?

> **To win and retain customer business, IT management needs to continuously engage with customers to understand their needs, communicate the value IT brings, and manage the IT brand proactively.**

The following sections take a closer look at how you might answer these questions for external customers, internal business partners, and internal IT partnerships.

External partnerships

After defining and identifying IT's value proposition, resources, and activities (scorecard goals), management may need to form IT partnerships with customers, outside consulting firms, vendors, or internal shared services to bring IT strategy to fruition.

Partnerships are driven by the scorecard, customer relationship type, and value proposition. For example, consider the following scenarios:

- If operational improvements such as reducing outages, improving system monitoring, and improving quality are goals, then Application Performance Monitoring (APM) software or vendors that provide test automation would be IT partners.
- If IT needs to provide personalized, white-glove service to the customer, then performing an outsourcing assessment to reduce costs makes little sense. Instead, IT needs to hire more employees or contingent labor.

Properly aligning external IT partnerships with scorecard goals ensures that internal resources create partnerships that help IT provide the agreed-upon value proposition.

Internal business partnerships

At a minimum, TSCs rely on internal business partners for financial assets, such as funding and allocations. IT also has relationships with business subject-matter experts (SMEs), who help IT implement software and services. These SMEs are typically superusers who help to support an IT solution after go-live.

After the TSCs, departments, and possibly the enterprise-level management identify what internal partnerships they have or need, management needs to plan how to maintain or develop those relationships with an eye toward ensuring IT delivers on its value proposition. To build relationships with internal business partners, management may do any of the following:

- Ongoing engagement, such as monthly governance councils
- Executive steering committees that ensure alignment with business strategy and shape the future demand for IT services with IT customers

Internal IT partnerships

Like IT partnerships with external customers, vendors, and business partners, a TSC needs to clarify its relationship with other TSCs, including details about services other TSCs either provide or receive. The goal is to set expectations and reduce uncertainty and risks.

Internal IT offers the greatest potential for economy-of-scale — that is, partnerships that reduce costs by leveraging tiered pricing advantages for licensing, outside services, managed services, and infrastructure. Also, these partnerships provide opportunities for employees to learn new skill sets, work on new technologies, and increase their end-to-end understanding of the IT landscape, thereby increasing the intellectual capital for the company.

However, like the relationship with external vendors, the TSC is a client of internal IT shared services and needs to establish service levels to measure performance because the TSC's ability to deliver on its IT promise depends on these key partners. These partners also compete for the TSC's business and are expected to provide quality goods and services for the money being spent, or they too could be replaced by another service provider.

Identifying the IT revenue streams

IT revenue streams sustain operations. In the case of IT, most cost structures and revenue streams follow a similar pattern: Revenue is the aggregation of all budget planning forecasts (in plan) and any fee-for-service allocations that the TSC can charge. Fee-for-service allocations might be project charges through a journal entry (JE) to a capital or expense budget as well as external fees billed for services rendered.

Although each company looks slightly different, all share common characteristics across their cost structures and revenue streams. Table 5-2 can help you determine potential revenue streams to support the TSC.

TABLE 5-2 Revenue Streams to Support the Technical Service Center

Revenue Source	Type of Expense	Examples
Expense budget (OPEX)	Employees	Salaries, management incentive plan (MIP), payroll taxes, benefits, recruiting, and relocation
	Discretionary	Training, travel and entertainment, meetings, professional services, licenses, dues, subscriptions, and service charges
	Semi-variable	Supplies, shipping and receiving, utilities, telecom, facilities, and maintenance
	Allocations	Monthly charges to business-partner cost centers for IT services
Capital income	IT-sponsored capital projects	Capital appropriation requests, such as upgrades, hardware refresh, or installing a new appliance
	Business-sponsored capital projects	Capital appropriation requests, such as internal company business initiatives
	Projects sponsored by external customers	External capital, such as projects sponsored and funded by the customer or client
Expense income direct from internal IT clients	Business unit cost-center expense	Work billed directly to a business unit's cost center
Other income	Selling services directly to external customers	Fee-based billing model: Technology, maintenance and support, or in some cases industry data

Although the OPEX budget is really part of the cost structure, it is also a fixed revenue stream for the TSC and the starting point to begin layering in other sources of revenue.

As part of planning, costs should be accurately forecasted for each category versus carried over from the previous year. This includes capturing any incremental funding (new capital/expense) for technology, outside services, or temporary staffing needed to deliver on scorecard objectives. For example, depending on your scorecard objectives, you might need to estimate costs for the following:

• Backfilling employees to prepare for an upgrade assessment

• Developing and rolling out a new SDLC program

• Providing user services, such as training or a superuser network, to reduce demand on support services

Developing a cost structure

Preparing the cost structure using the ITBM enables budgets to be based on the value proposition, not just financial targets. The cost structure is based on the decisions made for all the preceding steps in the ITBM process. In addition, the cost structure needs to take the following factors into account:

- Fixed software amortization, fixed hardware depreciation, and other fixed costs
- Money paid to shared internal services (IT or business)
- Temporary outside services
- Increases in licensing or maintenance costs

Cost structures establish controls for variable costs to ensure revenue streams and allocations are flexible enough to recapture these costs from clients.

Cost structure analysis is the last chance to look for economies of scope and scale, where business units can share people and system resources and thereby reduce licensing, hardware and support costs. In addition, reviewing all IT partnerships with external vendors ensures that the right controls are in place to reduce costs and improve vendor outcomes.

By now, the TSC knows whether it's providing no frills or white-glove service (or something in-between). Now, it's time to reconcile the cost of that service with the available revenue. Whether the business has money available for the desired service levels may depend on how profit-driven the overall business model is:

- If profit-driven is the decided approach, then the expectations around creating scale, growth, value proposition, and customer relationships may need to be lowered.
- If the business gives IT the financial flexibility to implement value-based changes and improvements, then OPEX budgets, new capital, and allocations back to the customer may need to increase.

TSCs must strike the right balance between the two models to achieve optimal outcomes.

To develop the right cost structure, the TSC considers the customer relationship types and value proposition it promised to provide to the customer. If the relationship type is infrastructure management or service catalog work, a profit-driven model can drive higher operational efficiencies.

However, when business units are experiencing significant change, growth, and introducing complexity, this work may not fit well into the predefined scripts that are typically used in a profit-driven model to deliver IT services. A dynamic business landscape requires an adaptive and tactical delivery model.

Chapter Summary

In the value-based IT approach, TSCs, departments, and enterprise IT develop a complete business model to identify desired outcomes, catalog activities, make investments, and establish rewards to achieve desired objectives.

ITBM enables TSCs, departments, and the enterprise as a whole to develop an IT strategy from a mindset that organizations compete to win and retain IT customers. Adopting this mindset and the ITBM approach is key to reversing the IT trends of failed projects and outsourcing.

The ITBM processes puts the destiny of IT organizations back into the hands of the TSCs by applying a bottom-up approach. As a result, ITBM drives more accountability across all areas.

Further, ITBM provides clarity about who the TSC is here to serve by ensuring that scorecard objectives, measurements, and exposure mechanisms are aligned with IT's value proposition.

Finally, the ITBM exercise provides a set of simple, common goals that everyone in the TSC can understand and execute. Moreover, these goals provide guiding principles that the TSC, department, or enterprise can refer back to when distractions arise. This new level of clarity increases the value that IT brings to clients and ultimately drives down total cost of ownership.

CHAPTER 6

SECOND PROTOCOL: TECHNOLOGY AND GOVERNANCE

Successful IT organizations all have two things in common:

• Clarity about their business model

• Documentation and processes to manage the IT footprint effectively

In most companies, however, the IT landscape (software, hardware, services, and resources) changes quickly, and a discipline for updating processes and documentation was never put in place or is only loosely followed. Employees may not know what processes to follow or must reverse-engineer systems and processes for every incident reported or project initiated. (That is, employees generate documentation as needed on the fly by logging into systems to document the configuration and design, or reading the programs, because historical documentation can't be found or isn't accurate.)

As a result, profit leaks that are hard to quantify drag down the IT organization and the business as whole. Further, maintaining good documentation on systems and processes is often not a priority, because teams are frequently understaffed and struggling to keep up with the demand in IT services. In that environment, it's difficult to maintain alignment between IT and the business model or to manage documentation that supports that alignment.

The technology and governance protocol helps companies overcome these problems by first documenting the IT landscape that's in place and then using that information to plan what the IT landscape needs to look like in the future. From 10,000 feet, the Second Protocol is a three-step process:

1. **Select an information management approach for organizing and updating documentation.** This approach may include a document management system and a learning management system.

2. **Assess the IT landscape.** In this step, IT management creates a topology document of the current IT landscape and analyzes what upgrades are needed. The IT organization also needs to develop a disaster recovery plan that documents all the systems' key dependencies and the requirements for bringing systems back online.

3. **Decide what processes will govern the IT landscape.** The IT organization needs processes for changing systems and how those changes are released and tested. Also, when systems go awry (because that's what system do sometimes), the IT organization needs processes — and the right departmental culture and mindset — for conducting root cause analysis.

Managing Documentation

IT's documentation (often called the *knowledge base*) should be organized so that support and project team members can easily navigate the documentation to find what they need. Today, a document management system offers the most efficient way to manage documentation. Of course, all the documentation needs to be available on the systems supported, so support and project team members can do their jobs, which is why I include a checklist of all the documentation an IT organization may need to create and publish later in this chapter.

Exploring documentation and learning management systems

A document management system (DMS) creates a centralized repository for all standard operating and escalation procedures required for delivery of projects, operations, and support. A DMS enables every team member to easily access current procedures, which streamlines their work.

To drive more accountability, a learning management system (LMS) can help ensure that employees and contractors are up to date on training for standard operating procedures (SOPs). The LMS tracks and certifies who has successfully completed online training. After SOPs are published to the DMS, an LMS discipline requires that all IT employees read or recertify their understanding of the updated policies and procedures.

Depending on the IT organization's size and complexity, a DMS may be as simple as a shared public drive with an LMS strategy made up of an Outlook workflow with email to capture events. At the other end of the spectrum is a SharePoint or SAP Solution Manager DMS and a third-party LMS tool.

When an organization implements an LMS, it's helpful to emphasize the overall goal: ensuring all employees understand how the DMS is woven into the fabric of the daily processes and drives value for IT.

Companies that embrace a strategy of using both a DMS and LMS create better team alignment; increase adoption of tools, policies and templates; and save time for resources by ensuring information is readily available whenever it's needed for a support ticket, project blueprint, or application redesign.

What documentation does an IT organization need?

Although each IT organization is different, the following checklists outline what documentation and SOPs increase the speed and quality of IT services.

Information management

Although the IT organization doesn't need much documentation for its information management approach, it does need a little documentation for managing its documentation:

- **A DMS strategy document** explains how the IT organization will maintain information.
- **An LMS SOP** outlines how are employees trained and certified.

Technology

To adequately document the IT landscape, at a minimum, IT needs documentation to track versions for software applications and modules, third-party adaptors, and software plugins installed, including schedules for end-of-life support and recommended upgrade dates. The following list outlines the documentation I recommend each IT organization publish and keep current on its DMS (unless this information is available in real-time through monitoring software):

- **A topology document** outlines what systems are part of the IT landscape as well as system versions and third-party adapters.
- **Server virtualization documentation** includes the CPU, memory, and DASD for each server.
- **Upgrade assessments and plans** list what patches or notes need to be applied.

- **An obsolete technology document** lists what hardware, software, or services are being decommissioned and when, such as an outdated ERP system or A2A, B2B, or third-party adapters

- **A disaster recovery emergency response plan** includes procedures and requirements for recovering IT systems after a hardware failure, power outage, severe weather, or other event that substantially interferes with IT systems that enable employees keep the business running.

- **A technology roadmap** explains the one-to-three year rolling plan for IT.

- **A development systems document** lists the tools and resources available for changes and upgrades, such as B-Landscapes, training boxes, and sandboxes.

- **System/Business validation procedures** outline how IT ensures each system does what it's intended to do and may include user requirements and hardware requirements discovered in the ITBM process.

- **The applications performance or real-time performance monitoring strategy** includes details about any requirements gathered or processes put in place to monitor system health and send alerts in the event of a disruption in service.

IT governance

Time is often lost when simple activities become complicated because roles are unclear or teams spin cycles because they don't understand the process for delivering their services. Further, when there is a high attrition rate of contractors and/or full-time employees, a blueprint for everyone to follow is critical. Therefore, in addition to system and environmental related procedures and processes, documentation of operation and services are needed.

- **A service level matrix** defines the agreements (the IT promise) between the services offered by the TSC and the time it takes to resolve Tier 1, Tier 2, and Tier 3 issues.

- **IT governance and change control SOP** for software development outlines the precedence, approvals, and required documentation to move change through the environment.

- **SOPs for responsibility on run (support) or operational processes** spell out how customers and other IT TSCs engage support. Include day-to-day SOPs for incident support procedures and prioritization of support.

- **SOPs for applying system notes and patches** explain testing, validation, and approvals.

- **Root cause analysis SOPs** outline the processes, documentation to be captured (templates), and reporting protocols for an RCA.

- **SOPs for developing test strategies and maintaining regression test libraries** outline a complete strategy. Testing software and configuration changes is its own competency center and requires end-to-end documentation, including when to engage with project teams to track User Acceptance Test (UAT) results and integration testing systematically.

- **System validation plans and UAT scripts for disaster recovery, upgrades, or regulatory requirements** include regression test libraries for all critical business processes. These libraries streamline the end-to-end validation of systems.

- **Development and configuration standards** explain the procedures for making configuration changes or developing software (code). These standards increase speed to market for future development and help support address system-related issues.

- **Portfolio and project management SOPs** include SDLC or ITIL/ITSM processes and templates. The project delivery methodology needs to outline the minimum requirements to move through the phases of delivery, including the gating and approvals.

Other documentation

In addition to documents all employees must read and sign, the DMS can store documentation about the IT environment and human resources to perform jobs. This documentation may include the following:

- Technical assessments of any kind (system, risk, disaster recovery, or upgrades)
- Workforce, capacity and demand management, and processes, including reporting, metrics, and tools
- Assessments for staffing, organizational modeling, outsourcing, or the skill sets required for internal employees
- Sourcing strategy and procedures

Assessing the IT Landscape

Before companies can publish documentation required to assess the health and maturity of an IT environment, they must adopt best practices for ongoing system assessments by providing a solid framework to enable good decision making around strategy, systems design, governance, and program management. Adopting best practices begins with an environmental assessment, which enables the IT organization to understand what the current landscape looks like so that management can decide what changes need to happen and best practices need to be implemented.

Unlike the ITBM exercise, these assessments are performed at the department level, where the responsibility and accountability for these factors lies and where decisions are made about addressing constraints.

Different assessments are required to plan an IT transformation or system change, safeguard critical business processes, and/or reverse-engineer systems to create an IT environment blueprint. Assessments are valuable for decision support, driving operational efficiencies, creating scale, and establishing better IT governance.

This section explores the tools required to assess technology landscape and ensure IT can meet operational commitments. Depending on criteria captured in the ITBM, each organization's needs may be slightly different. Therefore, I discuss three common types of ERP software assessments:

- System environmental assessments (process mapping and reverse-engineering)
- Upgrade assessments
- Disaster recovery application impact assessment (AIA)

ERP system environmental assessments

Maintaining an end-to-end system documentation and topology documents can be an arduous task. As a result, most companies let this documentation fall to the wayside due to more critical priorities. Eventually, however, when IT is no longer sure what the enterprise applications footprint includes, it's time for a technology assessment. IT needs to take inventory of its systems, critical processes, and supported interfaces.

In most ERP environments, there are best practices to reverse-engineer the environment, including programs that collect statistics and identify remediation services required to address performance and system issues.

In some cases, vendors can provide a service delivery assessment. For example, in an SAP ERP system, companies can request a Solution Manager Assessment (service report). This type of assessment can be more costly than doing an assessment internally, but vendors leverage a standard set of industry best practices that identify and highlight core business processes, their relationship to system performance, and areas for potential concern. These best practices include capturing critical issues and primary factors that negatively impact the operation of landscape components, interfaces, and business processes analyzed during the service delivery process.

The findings regarding core business processes, systems, and the solution landscape are based on the information provided to the vendor during the service delivery assessment. Therefore, it's important to assign experienced internal resources to the technology assessment to ensure the vendor accurately captures the critical business processes and technology dependencies.

In a comprehensive assessment, areas of concern are cataloged in detail and the corresponding recommendations appear in the report's executive summary. The recommendations include an action plan for next steps. After IT management develops an action plan, the action plan must be shared with the technical service centers, where team members are assigned to remedy the issues. Treating the action plan like a small project or creating an umbrella scorecard objective to address and track the corrective actions is a pragmatic, comprehensive approach for remediation.

The service delivery assessment provides the foundation for creating comprehensive business process reverse-engineering documentation as well as system environment topology documents. The IT organization plays an important role in building all artifacts to ensure documentation includes all order channels and critical interfaces, including A2A/B2B technologies. Although an assessment for each company may look different, every assessment should include the following key elements:

- Solution landscape diagram and narrative
- A list of systems and software installed, including a database catalog
- A list of hardware servers and related infrastructure systems (including virtualization)
- A diagram of critical interfaces
- Business process reverse-engineering documentation — a topology of the current system environment and the business processes it supports
- A list of issues requiring remediation
- Recommendations to optimize the ERP environment

ERP upgrade assessments

Upgrades, patches, enhancement packs, and notes are required to keep ERP systems running smoothly, keep them scalable, and provide new functionality that support business processes. When the IT organization postpones periodic maintenance and upgrades, numerous support packs or versions need to be applied to bring systems up to date. Thus, upgrades cost more (for remediation and safeguarding) and their complexity increases the risk of IT interruptions. Bringing neglected systems to current versions often requires significant planning, coordination, and validation because testing crosses many systems. Further, plugins and third-party adapters often require new versions to work with the latest release of ERP software. In some cases, the upgrade must be split into multiple major events and spread out over multiple years in order to bring systems up to the current versions safely.

For companies with severely outdated systems, an upgrade assessment provides the roadmap for the upgrade project and includes recommendations for how to reduce the costs of keeping systems current in the future. During this assessment, IT management works with other departments and technical service centers (TSCs) to confirm the scope; develop high-level timelines; prepare budget estimates; and identify risks, dependences, and synergies with other projects. At a high level, a typical ERP upgrade assessment includes the following types of activities:

- Cataloging all physical assets available (hardware and virtualization)
- Verifying what upgrade software (including the version) is required
- Cataloging all ERP systems, third-party adapters, and versions
- Capturing dependencies (RDBMS upgrade, hardware refresh, adapters, and plugins)
- Performing predictive analysis to identify the relevant business processes impacted
- Determining the approach (upgrade existing systems or create alternate IT landscapes)
- Determining the hardware and capacity needs
- Determining dependencies on integrated ERP modules (A2A, B2B, customer relationship management, business intelligence, and so on)
- Performing a technical and functional upgrade discovery scan
- Scanning ERP systems with a development code discovery tool (code remediation assessment)
- Considering economies of scale for concurrent projects (such as disaster recovery, a hardware refresh, or a major project requiring end-to-end system validation)

Economy of scale is achieved when dependent projects are planned together that require end-to-end system testing or significant system validation. Coordinating this testing and validation reduces costs, rework, unnecessary freezes, and the risk of taking systems offline multiple times (which keeps users from performing their work and hurts the business overall).

The following sections take a closer look at key activities in an ERP assessment.

Evaluating the scope of the upgrades

Each ERP application package may be different. Some vendors, like SAP, recommend installing new support packages at least annually to prevent problems that have already been corrected from recurring in the SAP solution. Enhancement packs are applied less frequently but keep the SAP ERP environment stable and deliver optimal performance. If the IT organization has been keeping up with these annual updates, a full upgrade assessment may not be necessary. Simply cataloging physical assets, ERP systems, and third-party adapters (if this documentation doesn't already exist) is enough.

However, when systems get behind, an assessment clarifies what notes or patches teams must apply throughout the year to address user and system issues. The assessment also helps IT plan for the time, resources, and risk associated with ensuring systems are current.

When ERP systems get too far behind on maintenance, potentially dozens of notes and patches must be applied during a single year. Every note or patch requires analysis, review, testing, approvals, and validation in production. Further, support organizations often attempt to solve problems by simply recycling the systems, hoping to reset whatever the problem is. However, this approach creates additional risk for business processes and interfaces.

One thing is for sure: IT can't put off upgrades indefinitely. Eventually the ERP vendor stops releasing notes for older support packs, requiring IT to update to the latest support pack to address any critical issues.

Communicating with teams and across departments

An upgrade assessment includes feedback from the all impacted teams (TSCs) including, but not limited to:

- ERP applications team
- Testing and QA teams
- Infrastructure team
- Vendor safeguard or remediation services
- ERP software vendor
- Managed services that are used or impacted by the project
- Project management office (PMO)

To ensure success, the upgrade assessment outlines how the project will engage all key partners regularly to discuss the project scope and how it impacts those partners. As a result, the assessment can provide detailed estimates and timelines for each affected area (or TSC). With these details, IT management can request funding for the upgrade project (typically a capital appropriation request, or CAR). After the upgrade project is funded, communication across departments and TSCs continues as the project is feathered into the capacity/demand planning funnel to begin simulating possible delivery dates.

Assessing systems with software

In some ERP systems, this assessment includes running upgrade discovery analysis programs and then extracting and analyzing the results. The discovery analysis is designed to compile and categorize potential upgrade conflicts.

Some ERP technologies offer prediction analysis tools that analyze how applying the enhancement packages impacts or replaces old functionality and what new functionality is available. Working with the business sponsors, IT management decides which new features align with the ITBM value proposition and the operational scorecard priorities.

Understanding dependencies

The upgrade assessment also needs to determine how upgrades will impact dependencies, with other integrated modules and/or capabilities, such as the following:

- E-commerce
- Business intelligence
- Electronic Data Exchange (EDI)
- A2A/B2B
- Customer relationship management (CRM)
- Supply chain management (SCM)

Outlining success factors and assumptions

The assessment should also recommend key success factors or assumptions about the environment and/or staffing for the upgrade project. It's important to set expectations with the PMO, management, and IT teams regarding the factors that can impact a smooth upgrade. Some examples include the following:

- IT will create a mirror of the production environment to perform a mock upgrade (proof of concept for planning the real event) to identify any risks or missed requirements.

- Sufficient technical staff performing the upgrade have the competency and experience in the current environment to prevent missed milestones, which create a ripple effect on other dependencies, such as support changes, freeze widows, and business critical projects that can all be delayed if mistakes are made.

- The project will use workflow to get sign off from each area (TSCs, vendors, business partners, and leadership) for key deliverables and commitments made. The executive steering committee will define and address escalations in a timely manner.

Mitigating risks in a large-scale upgrade project

After analysis is complete, the upgrade assessment provides the plan to mitigate risks associated with any major changes being introduced (such as other projects) during the ERP upgrade window. The goal is to reduce the re-keying in any alternate or B-Landscape created for the upgrade path or the need to synchronize the two paths to production. Changes lost (code, configuration, objects, or transports) lead to missed functionality when solutions go live after the upgrade.

To effectively manage all changes moving through the environment during the upgrade freeze window, the upgrade project team partners early and proactively with the portfolio management team to understand what key initiatives are in the pipeline. To understand the key initiatives, the upgrade project team tracks all upgrade prerequisite projects, such as hardware refreshes, Oracle (or other RDBMS) upgrades, as well as mini-projects to update third-party adapters.

When possible, the strategy should keep the predecessor upgrades separate from the timing of the main ERP application upgrade, performing each independently. Although this strategy increases the timeline, cost, and testing required, this strategy also significantly reduces the risk of extended downtime that upgrade back-outs can cause.

ERP disaster recovery Application Impact Assessment (AIA)

Like ITIL, ITSM, and strategic sourcing, developing a comprehensive disaster recovery (DR) program cannot be covered in one chapter. However, a practical consideration of the DR program is part of the technology and governance strategy for the Second Protocol.

In most companies, disaster recovery is not about rebounding after natural disasters or low-probability events such as widespread regional outages caused by fires, floods, earthquakes, and acts of terrorism. Most studies show that downtime is caused by mundane events including hardware failure, severe weather, or power outages. In fact, the number one cause of outages is hardware failures — not natural disasters.

Why do companies need a DR strategy? Failure to develop a comprehensive business continuity and disaster recovery (DR) program leaves companies vulnerable to risks, including revenue loss, penalties, and fines, as well as a negative impact to the company's reputation due to downtime, data loss, and/or failure to deliver products and services.

Therefore, the starting point for evaluating the existing DR strategy or creating a new one is to conduct an Application Impact Assessment (AIA). This can be performed by an in-house team such as a service continuity office (SCO) or by an independent vendor. Although many software vendors that provide DR solutions offer services for the initial assessment, as you can imagine, solution recommendations post-assessment are aligned with their products and services.

During the AIA, for all in-scope applications, a project team collects and validates information with a focus on key dependencies that may impact the recovery of the ERP environment. If a system environmental assessment has been performed and this assessment reflects the current IT landscape, these documents become the starting point for the AIA to catalog critical systems, processes, and interfaces that make up the scope of the DR program.

In addition to IT analysis, the SCO or vendor must meet with IT and business leadership to walk through the business continuity commitments for the organization, taking into consideration all factors including people, processes, and technology. For example, what is the business continuity plan if the system goes down on day two of the year-end close and what is the maximum time the system can be down before impacting the closure of the books for the year?

The following sections explain in more detail key tasks in the AIA process.

Figuring out requirements

Requirements are driven by all business unit recovery time objectives (RTOs). Is a 72-, 48- or 24-hour outage acceptable under some circumstances? For example, in oncology distribution, cancer drugs are expensive with a short shelf life, so clinics order drugs just in time for patients. If inventory is not available at a clinic when the patient shows up, treatments need to be rescheduled, and the delay may put the patient's life at risk. Further, when the wholesaler cannot fill a critical order, clinics buy from a secondary wholesaler instead, resulting in lost revenue. A 24-hour outage could cost the company millions in sales. In this example, the business may require a 3-hour recovery time objective (RTO) to restore distribution operations and begin filling orders.

These service levels can also be gathered during the ITBM process when defining the customer types and customer relationships.

Another consideration is the recovery point objective (RPO), or the maximum tolerable period in which data may be lost due to a major incident. With a 5-minute RPO, all orders or possible transactions during this window may be completely lost and cannot be recovered.

After the organization has defined the requirements, the SCO or vendor can meet with IT representatives (applications, networking, infrastructure, support, and operations) to evaluate dependencies and potential recovery alternatives that can be employed during a technology interruption.

Documenting the disaster recovery plan

The goal of the AIA to ensure the DR plan protects the entire business process. After the disaster recovery AIA is complete, the resulting documentation includes recommendations for the DR technology strategy and maps the critical business processes to the supporting applications and IT systems. An AIA should include a strategy and recommendations for the following deliverables:

- **A Disaster Recovery Master Plan** provides a structured approach for responding to unplanned incidents that threaten an IT infrastructure, which includes hardware, software, networks, processes, and people. Sometimes known as a DRP, this plan serves as a documented process or set of procedures to recover and protect a business IT infrastructure in the event of a disaster. The plan defines a consistent actions to be taken before, during, and after a disaster.

- **A Disaster Recovery Activation Plan** explains what triggers and processes are involved in activating the disaster recovery plan. Activation is the method by which the DR actions are initiated and executed when a qualifying event occurs. To ensure timely activation, related steps and procedures address all requirements, such as safety, chain of command, escalation, and effective communication.

- **Business Continuity Plan (BCP)** outlines how to continue operations if a business is affected by system outage resulting from a disaster. The BCP explains how the business would recover its operations or continue using a contingency plan. For example, a contingency plan might be moving people and operations to a new site or perhaps using manual processes to accomplish the same tasks.

- **Cyclic DR Exercise Strategy and System Validation Approach** provides a framework for executing DR exercises and system validation. This framework would include best practices on creating system validation scripts and managing test regression libraries.

- **A plan for restoring operations to the original systems** typically focuses on using a backup system. However, equal emphasis needs to be put on returning to the original source system, including the steps required to safely switch back after the problem is resolved.

- **A plan for continuous process improvement** includes SOPs for using the results of cyclic exercises to optimize and improve recovery plans.

Considering some lessons learned

If you are going through a disaster recovery AIA for the first time, it is helpful to gather lessons learned from other companies in the same industry using the same technologies. Here are some common AIA lessons learned and considerations for the DR approach, based on my personal experiences:

- The DR plan needs to include dependencies on other critical IT initiatives, like system upgrades or new modules. Because the DR project can span a year or more, teams should use the IT roadmap to work around system and database upgrades and be notified when new client/host systems are created.

- Where you locate the DR site can significantly impact your design. Generally, the farther one site is from another, the higher the delay in the delivery of each packet, or "latency." If your recovery site is too far away, your data cannot be mirrored synchronously (in real time), and thus, you'll need a data replication solution.

- Consider the pros and cons for how replication will occur:

  - *Synchronous:* Is a fully operational backup of the business system synchronized real time. Synchronous replication means that clients making changes on disk at the primary site can't proceed until that data also resides on disk at the disaster recovery site.
  - *Asynchronous:* In asynchronous replication, the storage system can commit changes before they've been replicated to the DR site. In a database example, the database considers the transaction completed when the data is on disk at the primary site. If a disaster occurs at the primary site, the data that hasn't been replicated will be lost.

- Even if your organization has SCO and internal DR IT services, also obtain an outside vendor estimate to have DR services provided as a managed service for comparison.

- Whatever the replication software vendor tells you are the system requirements for memory, CPU, and DASD, as well as the expected drag for replication, double them when provisioning the systems.

- For the DR exercise validation plan, do not just bring up systems and verify the targets are running. The DR validation exercise should fully test the backup system. For a distribution business, for example, orders should be created, pickers should pick using the handheld devices, and quality checks should be performed. In fact, take the product to manifesting (end to end) before canceling the order.

- Restoring to the source system (failing back over) needs to be included in the DR plan and exercise. The goal is to bring up operations (failover) and restore to the original production environment after the problem has been resolved. This should be part of the annual validation exercise to determine the best approach for minimizing lost transactions.

- Document how to troubleshoot and test the original source production system without impacts to the failover system. Ask how the support team will bring the original system back up and validate it before switching back over without impacting the backup system?

- During the DR build, plan for a performance test environment of the largest databases and applications to replicate transactional volumes. Often network latency issues do not occur until you cross a volume threshold. Benchmarking or using smaller databases or applications first can result in finding problems late in the project.

- Keep in mind that during any proof-of-concepts or when bringing up the new target, the system must be a clone of the production environment, including any system-level backend cron jobs and batch schedules. Ensure the DR system cannot trigger an event by accident, such as generating duplicate orders being processed or restarting loads from old batch events.

Creating a plan internally versus hiring a vendor

Creating and managing the DR program is a substantial investment in human resources to design and implement an IT recovery plan. Alternatively, some companies choose to partner with a qualified service provider to perform these tasks, because providing DR is not really in the catalog of products or services IT wants to provide.

In the end, the objective is to architect a DR strategy that instills confidence that systems are recoverable. The decision about whether to provide DR recovery services in-house or hire a managed recovery service provider comes down to a few key factors:

- Look for economies of scale and cost for managing the entire enterprise DR program, including hardware, recovery software, and joint DR exercises.
- Consider whether customers and business partners are comfortable with letting another group of individuals access your data and systems. If your IT organization fears the loss of control, then structure the master service agreement so that the managed recovery service provider operates as an extension of your IT organization under your guidelines.
- Finally, decide whether disaster recovery planning and services are a core competency that you want to staff and mature in your organization. Keeping DR recovery services in-house can divert valuable IT resources from supporting the organization's core business activities.

Developing Processes That Govern the IT Landscape

Remember that, in the Second Protocol, the goal is to make sure everyone in the IT organization understands the business model and what processes they need to follow in order to support that business model.

After the IT organization has a clear picture of the current IT landscape, as well as plans for upgrades and disaster recovery, it's time to develop processes that enable the IT organization to move forward with those plans and any plans that support the future of the business.

The following sections provide a blueprint for developing processes that manage changes to the IT landscape, release schedules, and testing. As part of this process, I also recommend IT organizations evaluate whether their organizational culture supports root cause analysis, and if not, helps employees shift the corporate mindset so that IT can use root cause analysis to fully resolve any problems that arise.

Change management

Change management processes ensure that code, data, configuration, and objects are migrated correctly and are accurately tracked from system to system. Developing a change management discipline establishes controls to ensure that changes to a system are introduced in a coordinated manner. This reduces the possibility that unnecessary or improperly tested changes create system conflicts or, in some cases, undo existing functionality.

Change management processes reduce disruption to services, reduce back-out activities, and ensure cost-effective utilization of key resources involved in implementing system change.

For purposes of this discussion, I also use an ERP environment as an example, because IT system landscapes and approaches may vary from company to company and even for each software application package. Here are a few examples of how an IT system might handle system changes:

- Some software applications include tools for collecting changes and/or transports, including the ability to manage migrations with automated workflow and approvals.

- Others use manual processes for importing, exporting, or moving changes from one environment to the next with manual checks and balances.

- In some cases, the landscape may include multiple layers such as development environment (sandbox for prototyping), a gold client for configuration only (no test data), and a unit test client.

- When multiple large projects are happening in concert, there could be multiple development environments and everything passes through a consolidation client on its way to production.

To illustrate the concepts I want to explore, I use a generic ERP landscape model that includes the following:

- A development environment (or environments) for configuration, and unit testing

- A QA environment for a second round of unit testing, integration, regression testing, and performance testing

- Production environment (or PRD), the final target where go-live validation is performed

- Performance environment (or TST), which mirrors the production environment that's kept in sync with all changes after being moved to PRD. In some projects, this environment can be used before cutover to simulate production and/or test performance before migrating code to PRD when required.

Moving changes from development to the production environment

Developing robust change control management processes reduces the risks and lowers the costs associated with managing ERP systems and landscapes by providing the discipline that safeguards environments.

This section takes a closer look at how change management oversees all configuration changes and how development code/objects are transported through systems from development to QA and onto PRD. When a system includes a performance environment, all transports are also applied to the test system after the transports are validated in PRD to ensure the test system stays in sync.

The reality is that not all changes require performance testing. In those cases which do, the changes may move to test before moving to PRD as required for volume testing or other validation not possible in the QA system. Figure 6-1 illustrates a typical transport path.

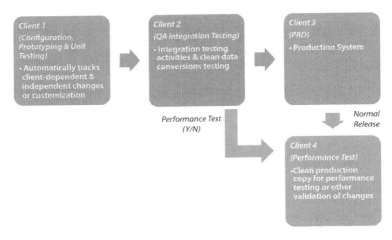

Figure 6-1

Although the performance test environment is typically used for performance or regression testing with real-life loads, the environment may also be used to verify missing dependencies in the production environment. These missing dependencies may affect how the new configuration or development (code/objects) works. In other words, when some projects go live before others, the code and configuration may test fine in QA because objects and configuration settings exist in the development and QA environments that do not exist in the production system (PRD). When in doubt, a properly updated performance environment that mirrors PRD for all configuration and function modules (code) can be used for pre-production testing.

Automating change control

Change control management software can provide automation to help effectively manage this critical activity. The benefits of using change control automation include the following:

- Every change is controlled from concept to test, and ultimately production use.

- Change control processes can be configured, implemented, and enforced while lowering the risks of users compromising or customizing the processes.

- The software efficiently and effectively manages and audits change release processes.

- Workflow built into the software automates change or transport synchronizations.

- The software reduces manual effort and significantly mitigates downstream risks.

- Human change/transport sequencing errors are reduced or eliminated entirely.

- Production system stability is significantly improved.

- Reporting for internal IT system change audits is streamlined.

- Transport history and logs capture documentation.

- Changes, approvals, and events are documented and tied to system users

- Streamlined processes reduce costs associated with implementing changes.

When choosing a software solution, IT must select a product that offers flexible configuration as well as approval processes. Here are a few tips and guidelines to consider:

- Generally speaking, the solution should be flexible and configurable to align with the subtle differences in how each technical service center manages system changes. The goal is to improve and streamline operations, not complicate them.

- The change request approach should be able to upload or embed all required documents (attachments) or document references (links).

- Look for software that provides integrated workflow with email alerts or reminders about work pending.

- Make sure the software can support your organization's IT audit and compliance needs, including enforcement of predetermined processes, segregation of duties, electronic signatures, ITIL, or regulatory required processes (SOX, FDA CFR Part 11, and so on).

Release management

Release management, in a nutshell, is a discipline for moving software changes from development to their release in production. As software systems, development processes, and resources become more decentralized as well as more specialized, release management also becomes more complex. You not only have to manage releases, but do so within the ongoing cycle of development and testing. In release management, a lot of moving pieces must fit together seamlessly to guarantee the success of projects and day-to-day operations.

A *release-management philosophy* is a standard set of repeatable processes to oversee integration and flow of development, testing, deployment, and support of IT systems. In addition, release management protocols establish a release schedule (frequency) and determine the cyclic maintenance window where changes are allowed to move to production and be validated.

Choosing who controls releases to the production environment

Each organization architects a program to identify, create, and/or implement the needed controls to efficiently manage the release of system changes or new functionality. Here are a couple of examples:

- In some organizations, portfolio managers oversee the release schedule and timing.
- In others, release managers serves as liaison between various business units and IT teams to promote smooth and timely delivery of software products or updates.

The portfolio or release manager is a gatekeeper who holds the keys to moving changes to production systems. Like an air traffic controller, this manager directs and coordinates this critical activity, including managing potential collisions between projects, such as an upgrade and project go-live schedule for the same release.

Scheduling the frequency of releases

An important consideration around release management is how often to move changes into production.

One school of thought is to allow major releases only monthly, quarterly, semi-annually, or yearly. In this model, all projects, and in some cases nonemergency changes, are aligned with predetermined cutover dates. By reducing the frequency of moving system changes, this model also reduces risks associated with making changes to customer-facing systems, such as a web portal, because frequent or poorly executed changes frustrate customers and increase customer care calls. For change-sensitive applications such as these, a quarterly or semi-annual schedule enables more proactive communication leading up to a major release, which reduces the impact to customers, users, and IT support.

However sometimes, IT needs a schedule that allows for more frequent releases, such as weekly, bi-weekly, or monthly. For example, for an internal ERP system, small changes like adding a new payment method or a collections process enhancement only impacts a small user base. Changes like this are not emergency or critical (like a break fix) but can drive immediate operational efficiencies. Too rigid of a release schedule hurt the business, whereas being too lax can introduce risk. Finding the balance between frequencies of moving change and establishing controls for validating the changes being introduced is key. Accountability is much higher when workflow requires electronic sign off for each stage of migration to another client.

Further, as noted in previous sections, the IT promise and customer type may vary from area to area. The release program should be flexible to deal with the distinct needs of each technical service center. Changes for EDI and B2B may need to be handled quite differently than changes for a customer-facing web portal.

Unfortunately, in some cases, organizations do not differentiate between the customer types of IT when architecting the release process, preferring a one-size-fits-all approach. When this happens, the organization might adopt a shared release schedule strategy based on time, typically in increments of 30, 60, or 90 days. The theory is that that moving changes less often reduces the risks of outages for all areas and creates economies of scale for testing.

Release schedules themselves do not catch, reduce, or prevent defects; rather, design reviews, configuration reviews, regression testing, and a governance rigor prevent defects. Reducing the number of go-live weekends does not reduce the number of actual defects that make it through QA and into the environment.

When ITIL, ITSM, and Agile are used for project delivery in concert with a fixed-release schedule, there's a risk that the release management focus shifts to managing time boxes for deliverables and go-live dates rather than ensuring the product's functionality or quality. Missing a release date causes significant delays because teams are not allowed to move the changes into production again until the next release cycle. Keep in mind, if this delay impacts business operations, exceptions are made under the umbrella of "off cycle releases." This, coupled with support, break fixes, and other VP overrides, leaves IT organizations already supporting a hybrid of a fixed release schedule and off-cycle release change management. The only difference is the additional paperwork to get this approved and the drama that ensues, including blame, criticism, and humiliation from requesting the VP override.

The other school of thought is that changes can deploy more frequently, such as every week, because requiring every project to synchronize to the same go-live date offers little economy of scale. In this approach, IT organizations acknowledge that exceptions are already made on a weekly basis for emergency transports, break fixes, and business critical changes that cannot wait, as well as off-cycle project requests as noted earlier.

More frequent releases address the risks of the fixed-release schedule (or sprint) driving the wrong behaviors — such as teams focusing on dates rather usability (value proposition). A non-release cycle approach with weekly cutover meetings and decision points takes the pressure off teams by offering flexibility to adjust timelines. This flexibility enables project teams and business partners to hit the pause button if needed and revisit requirements, perform change control for scope, or rethink functionality without fear of delaying a project for another 30-, 60-, or 90-day sprint.

In this model, teams are more likely to take an extra week or two if there is any uncertainty about the readiness for cutover, to verify and consolidate transports lists, or if additional user acceptance testing (UAT) is required before sign off. This extra time can reduce and prevent outages, thereby reducing additional costs incurred by hasty approvals to make the release.

Another prevailing myth around using a fixed-release cycle or sprint is that it reduces the cost for QA testing because QA teams can run complete validation scripts from the regression library for an entire area, like order-to-cash, procure-to-pay, or financials, one-time for all projects and/or changes moving through the environment. True, a fixed-release cycle does reduce duplication of testing for the same ERP transactions or functional modules. However, as discussed earlier, software development is not predictable. IT organizations typically don't benefit from the supposed economies of scale for the following reasons:

- The likelihood of all changes for all projects being available at the same time for testing is very low.
- If all changes are held until the end of the sprint, this can be problematic for the QA teams from a workload perspective.
- Development teams will also struggle to address all defects found during system integration testing if held to the end of the sprint to create economies of scale.

- Finally, when some projects have defects, others projects then become dependent on successful end-to-end testing or re-testing schedules in the shared test strategy.

In contrast, in the weekly release model, QA is responsible for planning and finding economies of scale to perform testing as code and changes move to the QA environment, which is more efficient for QA — and therefore less costly in the long-run for the organization. In this model, decisions on joint testing across projects are made on a case-by-case basis.

To improve the likelihood of success for the release management program, here are some key considerations for choosing an approach:

- How can the production system stability be significantly improved, or how can outages reduced by increasing or decreasing the frequency of releases?
- What metrics are in place to measure whether the processes are effectively managed?
- How is the release management approach reducing manual effort and rework or increasing the administrative overhead?
- How could human errors/issues be largely eliminated and ultimately reduce defects after go-live through automation and tools versus fixed-release cycles?
- How does the release management automation or workflow address all findings on IT system internal audits?
- How does the release management program consider cross-application dependencies and transport/change synchronizations?
- How can the release management program ultimately lower cost of ownership when moving changes through your environment?

Test Center of Excellence (TCoE)

A Test Center of Excellence (TCoE) drives quality for all IT deliverables across the enterprise by standardizing processes, centralizing testing resources, eliminating redundancies, and increasing efficiencies across projects and support. A TCoE maximizes the reuse of skills; leverages licenses, hardware, and common expertise; and grows the intellectual property of testing teams.

In other words, the TCoE manages the quality and testing program, and this program is at the heart of IT governance, because all major changes for the IT footprint traverse a QA environment, including installing new systems, delivering support and project enhancements, and validating systems for regulatory requirements and system upgrades.

Because a TCoE centralizes testing operations, the TCoE helps the business ensure quality by building a focused community of testers and creating a scalable model. The TCoE approach maximizes IT investments by providing end-to-end testing and reducing total cost of ownership. Specifically, a TCoE can offer the following benefits and efficiencies

- Faster time to market (through test automation and regression libraries)
- Higher accountability (through defect reporting and analysis)
- Improved quality (fewer defects through better test strategies and standardization)
- Better resource management (by providing scalability to grow and shrink)

The following sections discuss some of these benefits and how to build an effective TCoE in more detail.

Exploring the benefits of regression test libraries

A TCoE creates economies of scale by creating regression test libraries that capture and retain best of practice test scenarios for business critical processes. Consider the following:

- These libraries alleviate the effort teams would otherwise spend developing new unit test plans (UTPs) and system integration test plans (SIT) from scratch.
- Further, regression test libraries minimize the problem of identifying over and over the same business scenarios required to test functionality.
- The libraries reduce the analysis needed to identify test data for preexisting functionality (that is, master data such as customers, materials, products, vendors, and so on).
- The TCoE consolidates test scripts across projects and support alike to establish the gold standard for all testing and validation of the system at each level (configuration change, transaction, functional module, and end to end business process flow).
- In the right approach, a regression library is organized to enable QA to selectively test changes based on the level of validation required. Test scenarios can be selected for a single-user task or transaction, business process, or end-to-end testing of an entire module, as shown in Figure 6-2. In this example, the test scenario is order-to-cash with levels of validation.

Figure 6-2

Creating governance for a testing discipline

A TCoE is more than just test plans. It creates a discipline where IT delivery and QA teams develop joint test strategies based on the risks and potential impacts of changes being introduced. The TCoE embraces the use of a traceability matrix to track test cases back to requirements for the change.

By creating a TCoE and integrating it into the portfolio, change, and release management processes, organizations can more efficiently integrate management of project requirements, testing, and development to improve project outcomes. Organizations do this by providing a comprehensive quality and testing solution that includes products, experience, and infrastructure using a shared-services model with chargeback capabilities to TSCs.

Meeting auditing requirements

A TCoE discipline helps ensure IT complies with internal audit requirements, such as Sarbanes-Oxley (SOX). SOX requires companies to separate duties in the change management process. Simply put, the same developers and/or functional analysts cannot perform both roles on any change moving from development to production.

The TCoE discipline is important because, often, team members test each other's work instead of using a QA competency center for testing. However, this testing role can distract team members who are working multiple projects or support tickets in concert with this additional responsibility, resulting in less focus and commitment to develop comprehensive test plans. A decentralized approach to quality can result in missed defects and outages at the go-live point. A mature quality and testing program works hand-in-hand with the change control processes and tools to ensure all testing is compliant, documented, and archived.

Developing or outsourcing a testing center

Creating a TCoE reduces costs by developing standards, repeatable processes, and test automation protocols where possible. This can be accomplished in-house or a managed service vendor can be hired to develop and implement a program.

Outsourcing the TCoE has a few advantages:

- The right vendors can bring technology, tools, and new levels of innovation from their experience in other sectors to drive improvement across the quality and testing program.
- Outsourcing can reduce the cost of test resources from 50-75 percent and manage test libraries at a lower cost using off-shore workers.

However, developing and implementing a top-notch TCoE for the company still requires some in-house resources for oversight and continuity. Further, the initial development and updating of regression test libraries and scripts requires employees who are experienced with the environment and who understand the systems and the critical business processes they support.

Developing a successful Test Center of Excellence

To assess and pilot a TCoE, here's an overview of what the IT organization needs to do:

1. Identify a trusted partner (vendor).
2. Perform an assessment.
3. Identify high priority areas for improvement.
4. Create a roadmap and strategy.
5. Implement the TCoE into the change processes using a phased approach, to validate improved outcomes.

The TCoE team must holistically look at the quality and testing program across all aspects of the IT organization, including SOX, regulatory validation, system changes, upgrade planning, and the IT roadmap (including DR exercises) to drive economies of scale for testing and validation.

When selecting a TCoE outsourcing partner, the following are key areas for consideration around a potential partner's pedigree for testing services:

- The TCoE follows best practices and recommendations for engaging teams and building test strategies for their operations and/or projects.
- The TCoE uses test data creation tools and has expertise to easily find and extract test data from production systems for regression testing.
- The TCoE follows best practices and solutions for creating the needed regression test libraries, automating testing, and generating reports and audit documentation for system validation.

• The TCoE has tools and practices for benchmarking volume testing.

Root cause analysis

Root cause analysis (RCA) is a method for finding the true source of faults or problems in IT systems.

In an RCA, the difference between a root cause and a causal factor is important:

• A *root cause* is a cause that, once removed from the problem fault sequence, prevents the final undesirable event from recurring.

• A *causal factor* affects an event's outcome, but is not a root cause. Although removing a causal factor can benefit an outcome, doing so does not prevent the outcome's recurrence for certain.

An RCA normally occurs after an event has happened and is a reactive method of identifying event causes, revealing problems, and solving them. However, information learned from the RCA process can be used as a pre-emptive method to forecast or predict probable events before they occur in the future.

An RCA is a key success factor for any IT governance and quality program, as well as an instrument for evaluating the performance of managed service vendors.

Additional benefits of the RCA program include the following:

• Identify barriers and the causes of problems, so that permanent solutions can be found.

• Develop a logical approach to problem solving, using existing data.

• Identify current and future needs for organizational improvement.

• Establish repeatable, step-by-step processes, in which one process can confirm the results of another.

The following are examples of events where an RCA can pinpoint preventive actions:

• Major accidents or outages
• Everyday incidents
• Minor or major near-misses
• Human errors
• Maintenance problems
• Productivity issues

- Manufacturing or distribution mistakes
- Risk analysis or risk mapping

How does root cause analysis work?

In RCA, the primary goal is to identify the following:

1. What happened?

2. How it happened?

3. Why it happened?

Then, the appropriate team develops actions for preventing the problem's reoccurrence.

Root cause analysis includes documenting the nature, magnitude, location, and timing of the incident being investigated, including looking at past events in order to identify what behaviors, actions, inactions, or conditions need to change in order to prevent a recurrence.

Although root cause analysis has different approaches and various schools of thought, some common principles and general processes for performing an RCA include the following:

- A root cause analysis should be performed systematically, treated as an investigation, with conclusions and root causes that are identified and backed up by documented evidence.
- The investigation should follow standard procedures and produce expected outputs. These include defining accurate problem statements and event descriptions, because root causes depend on the way in which the problem is defined.
- An event or problem may have more than one root cause, so findings should be validated and the problem re-created where possible if there is uncertainty.
- To be effective, the analysis should catalog the sequence of all events using a timeline to clarify the relationships between causal factors, root cause(s), and the original event. The timeline helps to prevent a reoccurrence in the future.
- Finally, before RCA investigators choose an approach to remedy the event, the team must explore all possible solutions to prevent a recurrence. If several equally effective alternatives exist, then ideally the simplest or lowest cost approach is preferred.

Creating a positive workplace culture for root cause analysis

The risk with when developing an RCA program is that organizations have a tendency to react to incidents or mistakes. In order for the RCA to not feel like a witch hunt and threaten IT employees and vendors, finding the root problem cannot feel punitive.

If the enterprise IT culture does not tolerate mistakes or sacrifices resources to save face with the business, the RCA program will not uncover the true root cause. This will inhibit the organization from creating a forward-looking culture to solve problems before they occur or escalate. More importantly, the RCA will not reduce the frequency of problems occurring over time within the environment.

Instead, the root cause analysis discipline should bring people together to find a common solutions, rather than divide them. The following story illustrates the power of an effective RCA program:

> There was excessive wear on the Lincoln Memorial from all the cleaning required to remove bird droppings. The park service experimented with different cleaners and brushes to cut down on the wear. If a solution could not be found, over time, the ongoing maintenance and re-facing of the monument would continue to spiral out of control. The different cleaners and brushes didn't work, so the park service looked at it differently and asked, "Why are we cleaning it so much?" It was because of all the bird droppings. They put up nets to keep the birds out and it worked some but not well enough and the tourists complained about them. Then, the park service went one step further and asked, "Why do we have so many birds coming to this monument?" After studying the problem, the park service determined that insects swarming the monument in the evenings were attracting the birds. The park service tried different types of insecticides but nothing seemed to work for long. So the park service asked, "Why do we have so many insects swarming the monument?" They determined the bright lights that illuminated the monument in the evenings were drawing the insects. Turning on the lights one hour later each evening eliminated over 90 percent of the insects and the resulting bird droppings. The brushes and cleaners, nets, and insecticides all addressed symptoms of the root cause, but were causal factors. The real problem was the lighting, and after it was addressed, the problem went away.

While this story may be a myth (because it has been told many different ways, sometimes with the Jefferson Memorial and others the Washington Monument), the story is nevertheless embodies the spirit of the RCA philosophy: The most critical part of an RCA is choosing the right corrective action to address the true root cause of the problem.

In a more relevant and definitely true story, at a distribution center one morning, old batch orders were accidently but systematically submitted, picked, packed, and shipped to customers. Over $100,000 in product left the building on its way to customer sites. This meant customer service was on the phone all day attempting to recall the orders, issue credits, and deal with customer complaints.

However, due to the IT culture and desire for each area to end up wearing the white hat, it took 36 hours to find the underlying root cause because teams did not work together effectively. The team owning the ordering system took the position that we have no record of this batch being sent from the client. The ERP team knew the order was processed because the product was shipped. The senior management did not provide the needed leadership to get teams to work together on the root cause analysis.

In the end, both teams were right and neither were at fault. As it turns out, a DR environment was brought online for the first time by another group (during the work week) and a unix-cron job processed and submitted old batch orders to the production client. Needless to say, another RCA began to understand the controls in place for the DR project.

Unfortunately, in the process of performing the investigation over the 36 hours, relationships were strained between technical service centers, senior leaders and most importantly, with the clients of IT.

The moral of this story is that, in order for IT professionals find the true root cause, the organizational culture must promote unbiased investigations without fear of reprisal. Even the best RCA methodologies and intentions will not address underlying problems if employees do not trust management or each other. Further, in a blame-oriented culture, resources will not be forthcoming on the true circumstances leading up to the incident. In this type of culture, employees play it safe.

For an RCA program to work and not extinguish the flames of innovation, there has to be a genuine desire to find the root cause and prevent it in the future without condemnation, as well as patience to find it via a certain degree of trial and error.

Chapter Summary

This chapter explored how technology and governance protocols help companies overcome challenges by first documenting the IT landscape that's in place and then using that information to plan what the IT landscape needs to look like in the future. The overall process follows these steps:

1. Choose an information management approach for organizing and updating documentation.

2. Assess the IT landscape, including creating topology documents of the current IT landscape and analyzing what upgrades are needed. Further, develop or refine a disaster recovery plan that documents all the systems' key dependencies and the requirements for bringing systems back online.

3. Decide what processes will govern the IT landscape, including processes for changing systems and how those changes are released and tested.

Only after the IT organization understands its IT environment, upgrade plan, and disaster recovery plan can IT create processes to maintain and safeguard the technology footprint. Companies must establish the right processes for IT governance, including the following:

- **A discipline of change control to provide quality, testing, and governance programs:** Creating change control involves mapping the change control processes to ensure they are relevant to the environment, teams, and compliance standards. Putting change control governance in place includes making the needed investments in technology to reduce human error and ensure repeatable and predictable outcomes. In some cases, these investments might require dedicated resources to provide oversight for the integration and flow of development, testing, deployment, and support.

- **A release management approach that safeguards the production environment:** IT needs a holistic approach for managing the ongoing cycle of development, testing, and release across the project portfolio. Release management protocols establish the release schedule (frequency) that determines the cyclic maintenance window where changes are allowed to move to production and be validated. To implement release management, IT might adopt technologies to automate and enforce change control activities. These technologies, coupled with good IT governance, can enable IT organizations to move change more frequently if desired.

- **A root cause analysis (RCA) program:** This program transforms the RCA processes from a reactive method of identifying event causes, revealing problems, and solving them to a preemptive method to forecast, predict and prevent probable events before they occur in the future. Remember, root cause analysis should be performed systematically and treated as an investigation, with conclusions and root causes that are identified and backed up by documented evidence. Equally as important, the organizational culture cannot sacrifice resources when things go wrong, or the RCA program will not uncover the true root cause. This approach inhibits the organization from creating a forward-looking culture to solve problems before they occur or escalate.

CHAPTER 7

THIRD PROTOCOL: STRATEGY, PROCESS, AND RESOURCES

The Third Protocol provides a framework for digging a little deeper into the IT strategy developed during IT business modeling (ITBM), or the First Protocol. Specifically, in the Third Protocol, IT leadership evaluates the following aspects of IT strategy, processes, and resources:

- **Do the scorecard metrics used to measure IT's value to the customer actually reflect the strategy discovered and outlined during ITBM?**

- **Do IT processes for delivering value reflect the work and needs of different groups within the IT landscape?** The processes need to enable IT to meet the scorecard objectives, not stand in the way. For example, resolving low-impact service tickets may be scripted work that follows an ITIL-based process, whereas the system development lifecycle (SDLC) process for major upgrades or new IT infrastructure implementations may need to be more value-based and flexible — more like a dot-com.

- **What is the IT roadmap for the next few years, and how can IT make the most of its assets and resources in order to implement this roadmap?** Resources include both technology as well as human resources (employees, managed service providers, and consultants). When you progress to the Third Protocol, everyone —from IT leadership down to the employees in technical service centers (TSCs) — understands who the IT customers are, what customers need IT systems to do in order to facilitate their work, and what level of service (white-glove or automated) customers need. In the Third Protocol, IT management uses this knowledge to develop the IT roadmap, which includes not only the specific projects or technologies needed, but also a specific plan that coordinates how IT will implement those technologies. On the human resources side, IT management takes a close look at the IT staffing model, making sure IT has the staffing levels and skill sets to deliver on its scorecards and looking for opportunities to do the following:

— Build in-house skills and competencies to create continuity and ensure predictable IT outcomes.

— Create a more flexible staffing model that uses employees' skills to their full potential.

— Enable employees to understand and take ownership of the IT strategy and business model.

This chapter explains how to evaluate and design scorecard metrics, IT delivery processes, and staffing and develop a departmental culture that aligns the IT landscape with these assets, enabling everyone in IT to successfully and seamlessly deliver on the IT's promise to its customers.

Aligning Scorecard Metrics to IT Strategy

IT organizations want employees, managed service providers, and contractors to innovate around delivering value to the customer — not gaming the metrics.

In profit-based organizational cultures, workers and managers find creative ways to make missed service levels look good on paper, independent of the actual outcomes or the customer experience:

• In one example that a colleague shared during my research for this book, a support team revived a legacy incident-tracking system to keep a second set of books for tracking open tickets. Then the IT help desk technician closed the original help desk ticket in the approved incident-tracking system in order to meet scorecard metrics.

• In another example, a managed service vendor categorized incoming tickets as medium or low even when incidents completely disrupted IT service (orders could not be dropped or filled). As a result, monthly reports reflected no critical or high incidents that failed agreed-upon service levels in the master service agreement.

What drives employees to game metrics? Table 7-1 shows an example of an incident support and handling matrix for setting service levels with IT users. As part of the ITBM process, IT management develops and reviews a similar matrix for each TSC. Understanding the service level as it relates to value proposition ensures the support teams prioritize work within their queue and determine how value is measured.

Table 7-1

Ticket Priority	Description	Handling
Critical	Complete interruption of one or more important services for multiple users of any location with no available workaround	Immediate escalation and response • 15 minutes to respond • 30 minutes to alert remaining business & users • 4 hours to resolve
High	An important business service is affected and/or many users are affected - limited workaround is available	Hot hand off escalation to Support Team • 1 hour to respond • 6 hours – provide updates to business & users • 24 hours to resolve
Medium	Issue impacting one or more business critical services and a workaround is available	Escalation via ticket to Support Team • 12 hours to respond • 72 hours – provide update to user • 5 days to resolve
Low	Low impact incident, no critical business services affected or a workaround is available for all services and business agreed to schedule to restore services	Escalation via ticket to Support Team • 24 hours to respond • 5 days – provide update to user • 10 days to resolve

However, a matrix like the one in Table 7-1 is just a start. It doesn't include all the scorecard metrics IT leadership needs to accurately showcase system health and support team performance. Dashboards cannot simply aggregate information, like tickets closed or backlog, into operational reports, because the value of IT support services is too complex to explain in a couple summary slides and charts.

The time required to solve help desk tickets is not linear; nor is the time required to apply a patch to a server. Further, the duration of an outage caused by a software glitch should not reflect poorly on one associate assigned to troubleshoot the issue or the department to which the ticket is assigned. When teams try to identify the root cause of problems arising from interdependences with other integrated systems or teams, the process can sometimes take days.

Instead of using operational metrics to measure individual or team performance, IT management needs to develop scorecard metrics that drive improvement. For example, metrics that count how many tickets were prevented by solving the problem the first time send a different message about what is most important. In this approach, analysis and energy is focused on reducing repeat issues and preventable incidents versus volume of tickets closed or backlogs reduced. Ideally, resources are recognized and rewarded for doing root cause analysis to provide long-term solutions.

To balance a "cheaper, faster, or better" services model with IT's value proposition, IT leadership needs to free up middle managers from excessive data collection and unnecessary operational reporting so that they can work directly with teams to understand who is performing and who needs attention. In other words, middle managers need to spend less time on metrics and more time engaging with the team and clients to pinpoint the areas for improvement around people, processes and technology.

In a value-based approach, managers focus on real problems such as monitoring the systems and proactively notifying the users of issues, not waiting for users to complain. You especially want middle managers to respond proactively to problems with critical business processes, such as creating a sales order or dropping an order at the distribution center. Middle managers also need to know whether customers see the same issues multiple times and work with their teams to find lasting solutions to such issues. Hands-on managers can keep their fingers on the pulse of the customer and develop an action plan to address customers' concerns.

Team and scorecard metrics should encourage managers and teams alike to innovate while addressing the needs of customers.

Defining the right measurements is accomplished by following the three-step value-based process introduced in Chapter 3, in which the first step is to identify the desired outcomes. This approach keeps IT strategy front of mind as TSCs carry out their day-to-day work. The following steps outline how IT leadership can transform metrics as part of this value-based process:

1. **Identify desired outcomes.** Customers may want IT to be more proactive and reduce repeat incidents. To control IT costs, IT leadership wants to prevent repeat tickets on the same issues and reduce demand for support services.

2. **Define behaviors and actions.** This step is where IT leadership designs scorecard metrics that reward value-based behaviors and that also help control costs over the long term. Include metrics that reward teams and individuals for conducting root cause analysis, preventing system defects, and maintaining system availability. In this step, IT leadership also needs to consider whether user training and communication, processes, technology, or staffing need changes

or improvements in order to meet the desired outcomes. Later in this chapter, you learn how to evaluate processes, technology, and staffing in more detail.

3. **Reward and invest.** This step is about taking action on the findings in Steps 2 and 3. In the case of metrics, decide how to reward employees and partners for prevention instead of just volumes of work. Also, implement any changes needed, such as the following:

   – Real-time performance monitoring that enables managers to focus on system health and communicating with employees and customers

   – Developing communication strategies and training that helps customers use systems more effectively

   – Adding employees or adjusting the staffing strategy

Remember that preventing an incident or outage costs less than correcting it. Establishing the right investments and rewards are key to driving new behaviors and outcomes that reduce IT's long-term total cost of ownership.

Matching Processes to IT's Value Proposition

In the Second Protocol (Chapter 6), you took a high-level look at processes across the IT landscape. In the Third Protocol, you take a closer look at the system development lifecycle (SDLC) to ensure that processes and strategies for managing IT projects and operations are flexible enough to move with the times and enable employees to take ownership of IT's value proposition for customers.

When managing IT projects and operations, IT needs a flexible and adaptive delivery methodology — much like what you'd find at a dot-com. In IT especially, processes and strategies change rapidly like the technology and applications they support. Quality methods (such as TQM) and software lifecycle management methodologies (like Rapid Action Development, or RAD) were once seen as the future of IT, only to be replaced by another generation of best practices (like ITIL, ITSM and Agile). Those who have been around for two decades like myself have passed through countless promising software-development methodologies like waterfall, prototyping, iterative and incremental development, spiral development, rapid application development, extreme programming, and multiple spins on Agile methodologies.

Despite all the evolution in best practices, project failures continue. All these delivery methodology processes share a predefined set of deliverables that project teams prepare in order to implement, enhance, or maintain an application. To avoid becoming bogged down in a single methodology and — more importantly — to ensure that whatever SDLC IT uses delivers actual value to the customer, the delivery methodology must take into consideration the following:

- The IT ecosystem is a web of interconnecting and interacting parts.
- Internal and external factors (both human and physical) impact the IT ecosystem's health.
- An ecosystem whose community of technology and people is growing at an accelerated rate becomes more complex every year.

Ultimately, the specific approach chosen isn't what enables IT to deliver projects successfully. The key is to understand the value of each approach and align the strategy to support the distinct offerings of each technical service center

---

There are entire books on choosing or architecting an effective delivery methodology program to address all aspects of project delivery. These books address key success factors like such the DMS strategy, regulatory checklists, communication templates, change leadership processes, escalation processes, project change control, and so on. The key point is that the methodology chosen doesn't drive adoption and success. Instead, IT management needs to focus on developing processes that are locally owned and relevant to the TSC and that provide repeatable implementation methodology. With these processes in place, TSCs can streamline projects and lower the total cost of implementation (TCI). In addition, IT management must ensure the processes addresses all project dependencies, coordinating the releases of changes across the entire project portfolio. The delivery processes must include establishing best practices that optimize resource-management, capacity-planning, and portfolio-management processes to create scale while managing costs. A properly designed delivery methodology provides a project-management framework for small- and large-scale projects alike by enabling cross-functional teams and solution architects to work together and deliver robust and simplified solutions that address highly complex business processes.

As I discuss in Part I, adopting ITIL, ITSM, and Agile practices can provide a framework for a best of class delivery methodology, but when these practices are improperly designed and executed, project delays and loss of productivity occur. Additionally, aligning an entire IT enterprise to a single methodology is problematic when employees don't understand the relationship between the processes and the expected outcomes (value proposition). This approach results in silos and induces internal politics, causing projects to be over budget or fall short on promised functionality.

Attempting to adopt a one-size-fits-all service catalog philosophy cripples technical service centers from addressing each customer's unique needs.

Because most project managers and sponsors don't know exactly what the project's full scope or constraints are until they get into the requirements phase, the software development processes must be able to adapt project scope and timelines to ensure solutions meet the needs of the customer.

The methodology chosen — whether ASAP, waterfall, Agile, ITIL, or ITSM — must be easy to understand and relevant for each TSC while providing a seamless integration across the IT ecosystem, including shared services and vendors. To adopt a light and adaptive SDLC, IT leadership needs to focus not on standardization and burdensome data collection and reporting practices, but instead on the following:

- The SDLC is intuitive and easy to follow for the teams and the business partners alike.
- The SDLC does not require exhaustive documentation and streamlines getting requests into the hands of those who can provide estimates and proposals for solutions.
- The SDLC should provide a map that everyone can understand and follow at a glance without a company-issued, lucky astronomer's decoder mood ring.

The amount of documentation for local processes depends on the skill, tenure, and experience of the delivery teams. If the culture is cost-driven and modeled so that the IT worker requires the minimum level of experience to perform the role, then everything needs to be written down in detail for the IT factory worker. At the other end of the spectrum, when developing the skills of long-term employees or adding highly skilled staff, the development and delivery teams can have more autonomy to adapt the approach by agreeing on deliverables required to execute on the distinct needs of each project.

No single script, template, or standard practice is plug and play for every organization, department, or technical service center. For some areas, an infrastructure management model of ITSM, ITIL, and/or Agile is a perfect fit. For other areas with long-term employees who have tribal knowledge and a medium volume of projects, the SLDC oversight required may be light. A company may even have IT teams that use a hybrid SDLC, depending of the technical service area or type of projects and/or technology that the team supports. Ultimately, the project-delivery approach should be flexible enough to accommodate dependencies with vendors, internals TSCs, and internal shared services.

Developing the IT Roadmap

A *technology roadmap* is a plan that aligns short-term and long-term goals with specific technology solutions to help meet those goals. It can apply to new products, services, and processes, including launching a new technology. After performing IT business modeling and technology assessments, a roadmap is developed to ensure smooth operations. Business partners, portfolio management, solution management, and operations all collaborate to develop a one- or two-year rolling view on technology changes in the pipeline.

The benefits of developing a technology roadmap include the following:

- **Ensuring IT teams and business agree on the future needs and what technologies are required to satisfy those needs:** Solution or account management proactively engages the business to shape the demand for IT projects and services.

- **Providing a mechanism to forecast technology needs and a framework to plan and coordinate technology development:** To this end, the roadmap includes scheduled maintenance, like system recycles, applying major support packs, and disaster recovery exercises.

To create the IT roadmap, IT leadership needs to complete ITBM analysis so that everyone understands what are IT's key resources (physical and human), key relationships, key partnerships, customer segments, and value proposition. After the IT roadmap is in place, IT management uses it to prepare the IT cost structure as part of the budget planning process. Simply stated, the roadmap shapes the vision and approach of how IT products and/or services will create value that solves the client's business problems.

The IT roadmap is not just a technology assessment or the specification and selection of applications and hardware. The roadmap is the intersection between providing the value proposition promised, procuring and maintaining the physical and human assets needed, and coordinating the entire program with the project management office (PMO).

An IT roadmap is designed and implemented collaboratively with operations and project teams as well as the portfolio management. Planning includes simulating key IT-sponsored projects (such as an upgrade) in the portfolio management pipeline to determine what risks to mitigate, what freezes are required, and what impacts will occur to committed projects. For example, the roadmap shown in Figure 7-1 illustrates where developing a simple plan can help map dependencies and avoid midair collisions for projects.

Organizations should first define planned maintenance windows needed to keep systems running or to apply ongoing patches. Second, map disaster recovery and/or other mandatory or regulatory system-validation exercises into the planning cycle (IT roadmap). Next, application, supporting systems, and third-party adapter upgrades (captured in the IT technology assessments) are feathered into the planning cycle. Then a dialog can begin with the PMO for approved project work or introducing new technologies into the environment.

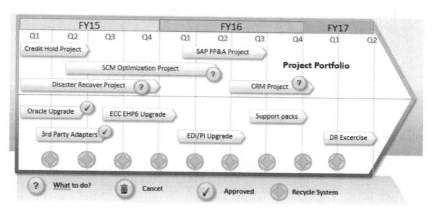

Figure 7-1

A typical technology road-mapping process has three phases:

1. Define and design.

2. Develop and build.

3. Execute and follow-up.

The following sections explain how each step works.

Define and design

In this step, the key decision makers identify what problems they have, their priorities, and how the technology roadmap will solve the problem. After completing ITBM (the First Protocol, outlined in Chapter 5), the TCSs should already know who their customers are, the customers' distinct needs, and what value customers expect from IT projects and services. This customer knowledge is the foundation for designing, developing, and implementing technology solutions that address business challenges around growth, transformation, and business-process optimization.

This step has three key outcomes:

- **Identify key partners both within IT and the business.** What groups need to be involved? For example, shared services, vendors, users, technical service centers and others may need to have input into the technology roadmap.
- **Identify leadership and sponsorship.** Before the IT roadmap is underway, company and IT leadership needs to understand the technology roadmap's purpose and value. This commitment ensures that IT leadership can request the funding, time, and resource allocation decisions that may result from the roadmap.
- **Define the scope and boundaries for the technology roadmap.** A vision for the business and IT must exist and be clear if the roadmap is to support that vision. If the vision does not exist, one should be developed and clearly stated.

Develop and build

During the development and build phase, the key decision-maker teams identify the critical system requirements needed to meet scorecard objectives. For example, improvements to the Business to Business (B2B) strategy to support forecasted growth of SAP ECC EDI volumes might include implementing a new SAP Process Orchestration module in order to leverage the power of SAP NetWeaver Business Process Management, Process Integration, and Business Rules Management. As part of the analysis, the teams evaluate alternatives, risks, impacts, and capabilities to finalize the technology roadmap.

To identify these requirements, teams complete the following steps:

1. **Explore what specific technology areas are impacted. The first step is identifying common product needs across the TSCs.**

When focusing on common product needs, teams can identify where the roadmap can follow a unified strategy that aligns the needs of all TSCs.

For example, to accomplish the same task for A2A data integration, a data integrations team may use multiple products, such as PM4Data, Informatica, webMethods, and Cyclone to name a few. Look for economies of scale to simplify the landscape and skill sets required to support the technologies.

2. **Catalog technology alternatives to address risks.** The teams identify the critical system requirements and their objectives (like reliability, performance, and/or costs). If there are multiple alternatives, critical variables are identified that will determine which technology alternative is ideal to solve the problem. Variables include constraints like time horizons for e-commerce that are relatively short or the ability to scale and/or handle end-of-month spikes in volumes.

3. **Create proposed timelines for implementation.** Finally, the proposed roadmap is feathered into the portfolio management to create a Technology and Portfolio Management joint roadmap. This joint roadmap is cascaded to the TSCs as well as vendors, shared services, and the business partners.

Execute and follow-up

After all key partners involved in the technology implementation validate the roadmap, the key decision-maker teams periodically review and update the roadmap. The technology roadmap is incorporated into the IT scorecards and reviewed monthly across the IT department. Progress is shared frequently with the stakeholders and business partners. Changes to the roadmap are well-documented and cascaded to all key partners, ideally using change control and workflow to confirm receipt and acknowledgement of any changes.

Evaluating the Staffing Model to Align Teams for Success

Providing all the services outlined in ITBM doesn't necessarily mean IT needs to create new departments or individual teams. In fact, IT may benefit from replacing rigid team and services verticals with a more flexible staffing approach. For example, the following list outlines the typical services in an ERP Projects and Operations department, where services are mapped to verticals and individual teams specialize in each area:

- Solution management
- Enterprise architecture
- Data management and governance
- Shared service centers [ERP, BI (business intelligence), EDI, EAI (data integration), and so on]
- Risk and compliance, including internal auditing services
- Release management
- Project management and PMO
- Account management
- Project delivery (may include separate teams for small and large projects)
- Support services
- Quality and testing services
- Infrastructure services (databases, UNIX, BASIS)
- Strategic sourcing

However, vendors do not structure their resources into vertical teams that provide only specialized services. If vendors did this, they would have the same challenges of creating scale and filling open requisitions that IT organizations do. Instead, vendors leverage all key resources across their companies, treating all W2 and 1099 employees as a large talent pool who can provide skills and expertise to fulfill client requests. With this approach, vendors search across the entire pool to find capacity that meets the client's need.

Another staffing model approach is blending verticals to enable more flexible staffing. In this model, the IT department is viewed as single delivery organization with both dedicated and variable human resources. A set of core competencies or roles are internal to the IT team, and other competencies are external. For example, IT might provide quality assurance and testing, BASIS, and security using a managed service provider, but this is transparent since both internal and external teams are blended in a strategic partnership model and follow the same processes. This will be discussed more in Chapter 8, which discusses strategic sourcing.

Whatever staffing model is chosen, it needs to give IT management insight into the available human resources capacity and manage the shared pool of resources. In this shared model, the company does not relinquish control, responsibility, or accountability for the IT services and project outcomes to a third party. IT and its managed service providers form partnerships with internal and external key partners.

Transitioning from service areas to competencies

In this shared staffing model, what was previously a service area, team or department may become a competency center. The model reduces the total number of service areas, resource managers, and associated politics to get work done. The goal is to map available capacity to demand versus debating who is responsible for performing the work._Everyone is responsible to help satisfy the client's needs. The reporting structures are not what is important, so the organizational structure is remapped into three basic verticals responsible for the delivery of support and project services, as shown in Figure 7-2.

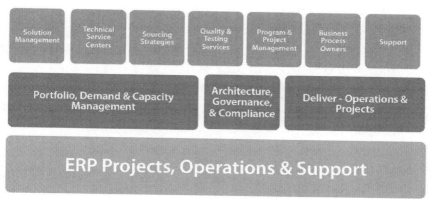

Figure 7-2

In the model shown in Figure 7-2, resources shift seamlessly between assignments, whether helping on a problem ticket or working on a major capital project. One benefit is that, even when there is downtime — such as waiting for QA to test, waiting for the business partner to perform user acceptance testing (UAT), or waiting for other TSCs to perform their tasks — employees with versatile skill sets can stay active on other projects. The goal is to leverage all temporary and long-term capacity for operations, support, and small enhancements by managing across the shared pool.

Managing employees in a shared competencies model

A competency mapping matrix, such as the one shown in Figure 7-3, helps managers coordinate their employees' skills and availability with the roles IT needs to perform. In Figure 7-3, if the reporting structure is ignored for a business analyst, the opportunities to fill demand go up significantly. With the right training and opportunities, the business analyst could fill multiple roles.

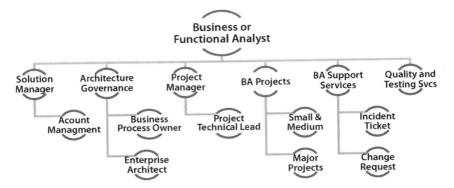

Figure 7-3

To map all available capacity to demand, resource managers meet regularly (at least weekly) to review shortages and communicate available capacity. It is critical that all resource managers attend capacity planning meetings because this is where decisions are made about new or temporary allocations.

Often, before projects begin, time estimates are padded, but as they progress, projects may go more smoothly than expected or use up all that padding and more due to unforeseen circumstances. Therefore, resource managers should double-check the actual hours booked in the work-force-management tool to pinpoint possible capacity that's not fully allocated or over-allocated. Also, resource managers should check in with their teams before these regular meetings to validate the hours actually being spent on assigned tasks.

Another tool managers can use to allocate resources is a capacity plan that enables managers see how an individual's time is being used. In the example capacity plan shown in Figure 7-4, what department this resource reports into makes no difference.

PROJECTS	Resource Name	Capability Area	2015–Q1		
			Jan	Feb	Mar
			Allocation in Percent		
FP&A Consolidation	Patrick	Lead / Project Mgr	0.35	0.35	0.15
HANA FI Reporting Project	Patrick	Business Analyst	0.35	0.25	0.10
Proposal-Credit/Collections	Patrick	Solution Manager	0.20	0.00	0.00
DR Exercise	Patrick	Functional Analyst	0.00	0.15	0.50
Proposal-MDM Project	Patrick	Solution Manager	0.00	0.20	0.00
Support & Operations	Patrick	Support Analyst	0.10	0.10	0.10
Admin Time	Patrick	Admin Time	0.10	0.10	0.10
		TOTAL ALLOCATION	1.10	1.15	0.95

Figure 7-4

This view at the resource level enables resource managers to pinpoint all capacity and map resources to opportunities. The capacity plan also provides intelligence to forecast shortages so that managers can predict when they may need to add employees, hire contingent labor, or increase outsourcing with managed service providers.

Whatever internal tools or off-the-shelf PPM products are used, they need to provide visibility at the resource, project, and portfolio levels. The goal is to separate the idea of a reporting structure from the roles employees perform in IT. There are some logical reasons to assign resources to specific managers, but from a capacity planning perspective, all resources are open game for any assignment. The key is to create one large resource pool for the application area while excluding resources tied to a specific statement of work (SOW) or master service agreement (MSA).

This model in capacity planning ensures internal employees and contractors alike are fully allocated by using something akin to Dr. Stephen Covey's Big Rock/Little Rock strategy: You put the big rocks into your plan first, and then fill in the pebbles and sand around them. The big rocks are the major projects you need to get done, and the little rocks are tasks like support and change requests. Keep in mind, the big rocks might have regulatory or financial consequences so employees and contractors must deliver on the commitments made. Resource managers track progress and communicate priorities weekly, adjusting allocations in a timely fashion if needed.

For a shared competencies model to work, managers, employees, and partners need to accept and support this model. To encourage everyone's buy-in, here are a few ways managers can promote why companies and employees benefit from this more flexible staffing model:

- **Time for improving processes:** When resources have free capacity, they can be mapped to augment support (except contractors whose hourly cost prohibits this). This temporary capacity enables support organizations to find time to work on process-improvement initiatives like user sustainment, root cause analysis on repeat incidents, or establishing performance monitoring with alerts of critical processes.

- **Opportunities to learn new IT or leadership skills:** Anyone who has a competency or desire to grow a skill set can get an opportunity to take a new role. Employees taking a first-time assignment in a new area can draw upon the expertise of the team to help design and deliver solutions. These opportunities create a culture of mentoring and expanding internal knowledge of systems and business processes.

- **Deeper connections between management and the work that needs done:** In the shared competencies model, everyone is a player and a coach, including directors and managers. "It is not my job" is not in the vocabulary of this delivery organization. As a former SAP Applications Director, I still worked on problem tickets, prepared proposals and estimates when needed, and ran projects when the department could not justify another full headcount to bridge the gap in staffing. When managers participate to support the operational needs, they keep their fingers on the pulse of the teams, culture, and customer experience.

- **Informed design and implementation of IT solutions:** Enabling employees to deliver a broader range of services can also indirectly improve IT's ability to meet customers' needs and improve outcomes. For example, for solution management and enterprise architecture roles, IT departments tend to allow only a few select resources or external consultants to develop recommendations based on industry knowledge versus internal experience. By keeping all resources (including solution architects) actively involved in the projects and support, teams build better and more sustainable solutions with support in mind. Further, when all resources recognize the potential that they might someday support the solution if an incident is reported, they're more likely to ensure the right monitoring and recovery steps are in place, reducing the transition to support time and warranty costs.

Despite the direct and indirect benefits of the shared staffing model, IT managers may still need outside services for support. As I explain later in this chapter and in the strategic sourcing discussion in Chapter 8, the key is having experienced support analysts who have tribal knowledge of the business. Also, as discussed earlier in this chapter, the support model needs metrics that place the value proposition over the cost of providing services.

Understanding what competencies don't overlap

Some companies that want to drive operational efficiencies may believe combining similar services at the enterprise level (project management, business analysis, solution management, and so on) can create economies of scale. However, this is often not the case.

For example, the network team operates very differently than the ERP applications team:

- Each has different value propositions, customers, key partners, and relationship types.
- Furthermore, for these two distinct services, account management and solution management require different skill sets and competencies.
- The teams operate under very different models. An infrastructure-management team is managing large platforms with high volumes and often

performing repetitive tasks. However, the ERP applications team deals with customer-facing technologies that require an extensive knowledge of the business processes those technologies support.

Companies need to recognize when departments do not share the same economic, operational, and cultural imperatives in order to know when to bundle and unbundle IT products and services, including the strategies for portfolio, workforce, and capacity management. One department may need standardization, predictability, and efficiency, whereas another is cus-tomer-centered, requiring a tactical and adaptive service-delivery model. The key is understanding the available pool using a competency matrix and not just mapping assets to an organizational structure.

> Sharing resources can increase capacity. To accomplish this, however, centralizing resources into physical departments is not necessary. Indeed, it is less costly to establish a matrixed framework across the enterprise. This matrixed framework uses a common set of practices to pinpoint demand shortages and excesses by skill set and competency area.

Creating the right culture for shared competencies

To allow capacity to ebb and tide with the changing landscape, organi-zations must be nimble and tactical. That means, to service clients, key resources can move seamlessly between roles, TSCs, and even depart-ments without conflict or politics. These temporary assignments are opportunities to strengthen collaboration across teams, grow skill sets, and increase intellectual capital in organizations. The obstacle is often not available capacity, but verticals in IT, managers protecting their territory, and other clan-like behaviors.

The key to optimizing resource utilization is culture. Resource managers must trust that sharing resources will not lead to permanent changes in staffing plans. Further, each year, managers need to believe the staffing assessment they perform will enable them to adjust headcount for the fol-lowing year. This adjustment includes actually increasing capacity if needed to fulfill the value proposition to which business leadership has agreed.

Everyone, not just managers, needs to embrace the culture of a shared-competencies model. Here are some examples:

- A solution manager or enterprise architect can be asked to execute test plans or perform validation on transports for a project go-live if needed.

- A developer can expand his or her role to perform business analysis or configuration, providing the controls are in place for configuration review.
- The functional analyst can be the project lead or PM (with the right training), create change-leadership communications, and serve as the solution manager to develop the design and blueprint when the right templates and oversight are in place for the competencies.

In this culture, IT organizations work as teams (or a tribe), not as individual contributors with different ambitions, seeking separate rewards for their own accomplishments.

Mitigating risks

One risk of using a shared delivery model is when the big rocks are pushed back because the assigned resources are spread across multiple tasks and their days fill up too quickly. Perhaps too many help desk tickets cannot be closed or a small enhancement takes longer than expected.

This risk of delays is why it's critical that managers, employees, and other partners see the benefits of this shared-competencies model. When they do, they're more willing to make adjustments, ask for help, or work a little longer during times of high demand. Without buy-in, if this model fails, the organization will return to the separate verticals of support, small projects, and major projects staffing models. In the old model, there are definitely winners and losers from an employee-engagement and personal career-development perspective.

Evaluating Staffing Levels

The customer relationship types (dedicated personal assistance, personal assistance, automation, self-help, and so on), which are assessed during ITBM, determine what skills and experience employees, vendors, and consultants need to have and how many people with those skill sets the IT department needs. The preceding section explained ways to optimize skill sets already present across the IT department. This section is about filling in any gaps in staffing.

Staffing assessments are used to develop the ITBM resourcing structure, including shortages and overages for each area by skill set, competency, and role. To ensure accurate staffing planning, organizational culture is crucial: Managers must be able report their capacity honestly without fear of losing headcount. To do this, capacity needs to be viewed through the lens of the entire application department, and not just one TSC.

Staffing assessments also consider the future need for headcount from capital appropriation requests (CARs) on major projects. Often project sponsors who prepared the CAR don't involve the TSC that will support the new implementation, and as a result, the CAR includes little or no budget for additional support of new solutions. In some cases, staffing forecasts are omitted on purpose in order to keep the ROI higher for the project approval. Therefore, TSC managers must proactively monitor the IT road-map, capital projects, and user growth to forecast the headcount needed to deliver and support projects.

To ensure TSCs are staffed to handle the peaks in demand, managers should be asking the following questions:

- Is there a major go-live of a new module?
- Are team members going to be required for an upgrade or a disaster recovery exercise?
- What scorecard objectives has the TSC signed up for, and what tempo-rary staffing might be needed to meet these objectives?
- What new technologies are on the horizon for the TSC (HANA, process orchestration for B2B, new OLAP/ETL tools for business intelligence, and so on)?
- What changes are coming as part of any strategic sourcing strategy?
- What are the company's targets for business growth and how will this impact support?

As IT progresses through the protocols after ITBM, managers need to continually assess whether they'll need to adjust headcount either temporarily or long-term.

Although ITBM provides a solid foundation for answering these questions, managers need to keep an eye on these issues not only as IT managers progress through the protocols, but also on an ongoing basis, because pri-orities shift, projects are delayed, and services required increase sometimes due to seasonal spikes in demand.

Building an In-House Consulting Competency

Consultative skills are typically sourced externally and temporarily for complex projects with the assumption that, after the solution is built, orga-nizations will not require this level of expertise in-house for the long term. However, the business is never static and always has a demand for consult-ing services.

Further, relying on external consultants puts the business at risk. As Steven Scott Phillips points out in his book, *Control Your ERP Destiny*, "Without a credible knowledge worker (the business analyst), the risk is that system requirements are shaped solely by current operating paradigms, user whims, and the department silos. When this occurs, you are automating the mess you already have." Building consulting talent in-house mitigates risks that external software vendors or consulting firms will find solutions based on their financial rewards versus what's best for the client.

The following sections explore what in-house consultants do and how they benefit the business. This includes ways to transition from external to in-house consulting and continue growing and developing in-house consulting talent.

Understanding what in-house consultants do

In-house business analysts are on the front lines to consistently and reliably meet and exceed customers' expectations. In this role, employees analyze and map business processes to design or redesign solutions. In-house business analysts have internal knowledge that enables them to consider the minimum changes required to systems and supporting processes. These resources are also more motivated than external consultants to look deeper at all factors around cost of ownership, including customization, software integration, hardware, licensing, and support to ensure these are properly weighted in the proposed solution.

However, business analysis is only half of the consulting competency needed. Because most ERP software can be configured to reduce customization for each organization, companies also need employees with the skills of a functional analyst. In-house functional analysts understand the business, its application software, where the data is, what the data means, and the data's relationship to the critical business processes. Functional analysts translate ideas into solutions by configuring the software application.

In my former role as applications director, I used a military analogy to explain what is expected of the internal IT consultant. Like the Navy Seals, IT business system consultants can be dropped into a hot landing zone (IT project) with nothing but a knife and a canteen and expected to execute on the mission. It doesn't matter what project, what technology, what ERP module or third-party software is being used. Platinum consultants learn how adapt and serve as a bridge between the business and IT to gather requirements, analyze the processes, synthesize information, and ultimately architect solutions for business partners on any problem they have. These solutions could be as simple as recommending new pricing solution for a product launch or as complex as a specification and selection assessment for implementing a module, such as CRM or SCM APO.

The in-house IT consultant competency combines the skills of a business analyst and a functional analyst. Employees in this role have a consultative mindset and engage with IT customers to understand the business needs and architect solutions that solve business problems

---

Discovering the benefits of in-house consulting

In addition to mitigating risks, developing in-house consulting skills helps to lower the overall cost of IT services. Consultants and business analysts are by far the largest outside service expense in the IT organization — and thus the largest opportunity to reduce costs by bringing this skill set in-house.

When a company has full-time, in-house consulting skills, it's also better positioned to improve processes and drive efficiencies. Consider the following:

- Companies using the matrixed staffing strategy discussed earlier in this chapter recognize that during low demand for projects or enhancements, these consultants can look internally to drive operational efficiencies around test automation, governance, monitoring, help desk ticket root cause analysis, and user sustainment.

- Because users change jobs, new employees are being hired, and solutions are often enhanced, there is always a need to work more closely with the user community to develop and provide better training. In other words, engage users to improve their competency with the technology and drive down the demand for support services.

- Another role for internal consultants is working with the business and the customers proactively to shape the demand for IT services by keeping customers informed of industry changes, new functionality, or new modules that can solve old business problems with somewhat turnkey solutions. Like the external consultants and software vendors, the internal consultant engages business partners proactively to sell the value IT brings and make recommendations for how the client can make investments to implement new features and capabilities. For example, internal consultants might recommend new plug-ins for supply chain optimization or an integrated module for contract management.

> In the long run, the cost of building or hiring consulting talent in-house is offset by the revenue and savings created for IT. In addition, customer satisfaction increases, the IT brand is improved, and building the competency in-house provides employees with a career path so that they can grow their mastery.

Transitioning to in-house consulting

Relying heavily on external consultants for projects creates a dynamic that is difficult to escape from:

- First, rolling off long-term contractors makes business partners and some IT employees uneasy.
- Second, using contractors denies internal employees the chance to build new skill sets and leaves them playing second fiddle to outside services on key initiatives. Employees may feel frustration, resentment, and apathy when contractors get high-profile projects, leaving internal employees focused mostly on support or small enhancements.

To transition from outside consulting to in-house consulting, organizations need to embed full-time employees on major projects as technical leads so that employees — not the consultants — become the face of the business's IT leadership. However, building the in-house consulting competency might require investments in training, giving trainees hands-on project time developing policies and procedures, and mentoring.

Training and project opportunities

Business analyst training is the first building block for a long-term strategy to reduce costs and roll off higher-paid contractors. Training also provides three key ingredients (autonomy, mastery, and purpose) required to motivate employees, as Daniel H. Pink notes in his book, *Drive: The Surprising Truth about What Motivates Us.*

The training content should be customized so that it's relevant and tailored to the organization's needs. To accomplish this, IT management can schedule workshops with instructors to acclimate them to the culture and internal processes. When possible, employees should be colocated for workshops that range from 3-4 days consecutively and that are structured into groups of four people who work together as small teams to complete assignments. These groups provide the added benefit of networking as well as building trust and collaboration across the teams.

Keep in mind, developing an in-house consulting competency applies to all TCSs including EDI, development, EAI, and so on. Therefore, companies should set aside time with managers and employees to understand the competencies, skill sets, and appropriate training required to address their demands. As a general rule, the business analyst training program should focus at least on three primary areas:

- Fundamentals of business analysis
- Requirements gathering
- Project management

In addition to training, some staffing investments might be required, including temporary contractors to backfill internal resources so trainees can participate in training uninterrupted and begin working on projects.

Policies and procedures

Standard processes, templates, and cyclic reviews provide clarity and prevent teams from spinning cycles and reworking problematic deliverables. To build in-house consulting, IT leadership and managers need to develop standard operating procedures (SOPs) for escalating and removing roadblocks when collaborating with managed service providers or across shared services departments.

The value is in defining and building a consistent set of skill sets expected from the resources and providing a framework to achieve this.

The Second Protocol, covered in Chapter 6, helps lay the groundwork for developing processes and SOPs that govern the IT landscape.

Mentoring

In addition to mentoring that employees may receive as they work on projects, companies may consider offering a formalized mentoring program as part of (or in addition to) the training program.

For example, BMW offers an apprentice program it calls STEP. During this 20-week program, candidates are paired with a local area BMW dealer and receive mentor-guided as well as on-the-job training. Upon graduation, trainees work full-time at an assigned local BMW Center, making a professional living as a BMW service technician. As a STEP student, one can expect an unsurpassed technical education and a career opportunity that comes once in a lifetime. Thousands of BMW STEP graduates have become well-compensated, successful technicians, body and paint specialists, shop foreman, service advisors, service managers, and industry professionals.

The IT consultant competency warrants a similar apprentice program because these individuals play a vital role in the organization by leading IT and business teams alike to translate strategic goals into tactical IT solutions. This investment reduces future development delivery costs, increases speed-to-market for solutions, and increases the overall delivery success. Further, a strong internal consulting footprint is the cornerstone to successfully implementing and providing oversight of a managed services strategy (outsourcing).

Incorporating in-house consulting into a shared-competency staffing model

Some companies might choose to create a core team of business-process experts (consultants) to bridge the gap between information technology, the applications team, and business professionals. In this model, the cream of the crop are selected from internal teams or hired externally. Often these experts are put together in a vertical organization and called a business process expert (BPX), solution manager, or enterprise architect. Their roles typically include responsibility for the development, maturity, and adoption of best practices where needed for the delivery of software application programs, solutions and projects.

However, I advocate that the consulting expertise remain part of the delivery teams and that resources participate throughout the delivery cycle, even taking on specific delivery tasks where possible. When making important decisions about the future landscape, the in-house consultant shouldn't be academic or just develop design recommendations based on theories. These experts should have real-life experience working with the business partners, users, shared services, and support teams in order to design flexible and sustainable solutions.

Ideally, the in-house consultant is a role many can play, not a position in a siloed department. Concentrating this skill set in a single team creates bottlenecks for initial proposals, blueprints, and estimates. When the ability to scale the solution management services hinges on just a few people, they cannot staff for peak demands. However, when the consulting path seems open to employees with varied skill sets, these risks are minimized, and the IT department promotes the idea of growing these skills across the organization and giving employees a career path to build mastery in their role.

Another way to incorporate in-house consulting into the staffing model is by establishing a business process owner (BPO) program. Employees who are a part of this program are responsible for defining processes, best practices, and SOPs and providing oversight of internal and external resources alike for an assigned area, such as order-to-cash, finance, procure-to-pay,

B2B (EDI), or development. Depending on the company structure and the staffing, a BPO program could be expanded for business intelligence, WEB, customer relationship management, and so on.

Keep in mind that BPO doesn't involve creating new positions or a separate department, but rather creating roles and competencies within existing job families, such as business analyst and developer. The BPOs are selected and an allocation is made in capacity planning for their time to ensure the needed bandwidth to provide oversight and governance for their stream. After these allocations are made, additional staffing may be needed to backfill employees' prior responsibilities.

A BPO program provides employees an opportunity to develop consulting expertise and improves IT governance, thereby reducing risks for change moving through the environment. In addition, the BPO establishes and oversees the controls that prevent bad decisions or poorly thought out solutions.

Growing the internal consultant skill set and establishing the BPO program also benefits large business transformational initiatives (BTIs). When external consultants with no tribal knowledge of the organization perform BTI assessments, the consultants' recommendations tend to map solutions into a predetermined framework that the vendors are familiar with or have used before at other companies — in some cases, whatever is the new hot-button method, like Cloud, SaaS, managed services, ITIL, ITSM, Agile, or running your company like a factory to name a few. By growing the consultant competency internally and using consultants in the role they were intended (expert advice), the risks and costs for IT transformations can be reduced. Before this can happen, the model needs to change where the internal business analysts are no longer overshadowed by external experts driving assessments. Using internal BPOs ensures that the IT transformation criteria takes into account the need for changes in all policies, procedures, workflow, responsibilities, and performance measures as well as technology. Keeping in mind that, when implementing software packages, consulting and professional services are the highest expenditure. Companies can embed internal technical resources on these assessments to ensure the right questions get asked and answered:

- What is the expected utilization of the vendor for the implementation? Who will be doing the configuration and development?
- What implementation strategies and methodologies are native to the software, application, and new tools/methodologies being deployed?
- What is the strategy for knowledge transfer and keeping the intellectual property in-house?

- What business reengineering will be required?
- Is the software or code proprietary and what long-term support agreements will be needed?
- What are the long-term support considerations for the proposed changes or new functionality? For example:
  — What monitoring does the company require?
  — What documentation is needed for the support team?

Success of the internal IT consultant depends on having a common set of tools and disciplines to ensure high-quality outcomes. When teams share a common culture, beliefs, and best practices, they develop an IT brand that provides a repeatable, predictable, and enjoyable experience for customer.

Chapter Summary

Just to recap, in the Third Protocol, IT leadership evaluates the following aspects of IT strategy, processes, and resources:

- **Do the scorecard metrics used to measure IT's value to the customer actually reflect the strategy discovered and outlined during ITBM?** Profit-based metrics drive employees to game metrics. In contrast, understanding the service level as it relates to IT's value proposition ensures that support teams prioritize work within their queue and determine how value is measured.

- **Do IT processes for delivering value reflect the work and needs of different groups within the IT landscape?** The processes need to enable IT to meet the scorecard objectives, not stand in the way. To ensure processes are enabling, companies should look within the organization to architect the best SDLC/ITIL approach before turning to outside consulting. IT management needs to understand each TSC's local delivery processes first and then look for broader synergies in the IT organization instead of using a top-down approach. Overall, the SDLC design should be driven by value-based criteria, keeping in mind "whom IT is here to serve."

- **What is the IT roadmap for the next few years, and how can IT make the most of its assets and resources in order to implement this roadmap?** The IT roadmap includes not only the specific projects or technologies needed, but also a specific plan that coordinates how IT will implement those technologies.

- **How can the staffing model become more flexible to help meet shifting needs for skill sets and to provide employees with opportunities to develop their skills?** Headcount and skill sets aren't all that matter. The staffing strategy must align with the organization's values, making it simple for everyone to understand the goals such as customer satisfaction, innovation, urgency, passion, or quality. This includes promoting a philosophy of one team, no silos, and no politics. Employees must have clarity of what is expected and how it is measured to ensure high standards, high performance, and an environment where resources are always improving.

- **How can IT develop internal experts to solve business problems and ensure that IT is supported and accountable for outcomes?** An in-house consulting competency (business analysis and/or a BPO) is better poised to understand the distinct wants and needs of the business and IT. Further, leveraging in-house expertise creates a culture where employees feel valued, respected, and appreciated, creating a higher commitment for the transformation. Remember, resistance to change is often a fear-based reaction and can increase the cost of solutions when the business needs are not clearly understood and internal IT is not included in the problem-solving exercise.

CHAPTER 8

FOURTH PROTOCOL: IT STRATEGIC SOURCING

Over the last decade, the demand for strategic sourcing has grown rapidly as the IT industry has embraced outsourcing trends. In the December 2013 issue of *CIO*, in the article "CIOs Opting for IT Contractors over Hiring Full-Time Staff," Sharon Florentine explores how CIOs are increasingly hiring more skilled IT contractors than internal employees. Among 84 CIOs Florentine interviewed, many were reluctant to hire and eager to contract. Two-thirds of the CIOs interviewed said their aging, legacy infrastructure made it difficult to implement new technologies, and that they don't have the budget or staff to hire new, full-time employees or invest in updated infrastructure. Instead, the strategy is to keep internal IT staffing budgets flat while increasing budgets for contract spending and bringing in more outside services and outsourcing with the hope of squeezing additional value out of existing technology platforms. In this model, strategic sourcing becomes the art of maximizing the dollars spent while managing expected outcomes.

However, this strategy may not take into account long-term costs, including the following:

- Costs incurred down the line to support systems that outsourcing partners implemented.
- Costs due to misalignment between the outsourcing partners' processes and deliverables and the company's overall IT strategy.
- Extra charges due to rework or metrics that weren't structured for a mutually beneficial partnership in the first place.

However, in a value-based IT model, companies use outside services in cosourced delivery models or strategic partnerships to create joint account-ability and responsibility for outcomes. In other words, the client and the vendor deliver projects and services together with the client remaining in control. In a value-based strategic sourcing model, the business can achieve the following benefits:

- Keeping intellectual property in-house, while creating meaningful jobs for employees

- Using internal employees to engage business partners, so internal IT employees remain the face to the business

- Increasing trust, thereby removing roadblocks with stakeholders and management

- Leveraging internal knowledge of business processes to increase speed-to-market

- Ensuring supportability is considered as projects are designed and implemented

- Enabling vendors to focus on providing scale and bringing new levels of innovation

Strategic sourcing means different things in different companies and can include or exclude certain practices. For purposes of this book, *strategic sourcing* is defined as the assessment, procurement, and oversight pro-cesses established to continuously evaluate and improve the purchasing activities of a company (as related to IT). This chapter focuses specifically on contracting IT work to a third party. In this chapter, I explain how IT can create an overall strategic sourcing plan, strategy, and oversight for its stra-tegic sourcing needs. At the end of this chapter, a case study from my own experience illustrates how I turned a profit-based strategic sourcing model into a value-based one.

Introducing the Strategic Sourcing Process

No matter the breadth of the required services, strategic sourcing starts with developing a plan to catalog and organize all required sourcing activi-ties, including capturing specific details of tactical and operational informa-tion, such as the following:

- The sourcing team responsible for each event, such as a project, service, or IT initiative

- Each step to deliver a sourcing solution (such as RFI, RFP, and RFQ) and the requirements for procurement of each solution, including the approach for capturing specifications for all services or products

- Defining a cost model that includes the upper and lower boundaries for the services' overall cost as well as the expected rate cards for a service solution provider
- Standard metrics for evaluating vendor performance

The sourcing plan manages the time and quality of the all events in the strategic sourcing program. To choose strategic sourcing partners wisely, IT management needs to analyze what services the business needs and research service providers. The analysis includes evaluating alternate possible outcomes and selecting those that yield the best solution. Then, IT management can evaluate different procurement possibilities while considering the value proposition of global service providers, specific industry conditions, and individual vendor conditions. Ultimately the goal is to identify the best candidates to address the organization's sourcing goals.

Typically, planning, analyzing, and implementing an organization's strategic sourcing includes the following steps:

1. **Assess the company's current spending.** In ITBM, the business determines what service levels support IT's value proposition, such as white-glove service for certain legal obligations or automated service for tier-one support. In the Second and Third Protocols, the IT organization determines what resources or skill sets are needed to provide those services. Here, IT leadership also evaluates what strategic sourcing services are currently being bought, where, and at what price.

2. **Assess the supply market.** Who offers what services? Be sure to consider boutique service providers as an alternative to the big names, such as IBM, Deloitte, Accenture, and so on.

3. **Analyze the total cost for services**. Research the cost of the IT services in similar industries (such as banking or life sciences) to compare both costs and approach. Build out pricing models during the specification and selection using a set of common key performance indicators.

4. **Identify suitable suppliers.** Because each business's needs are unique, assessing a specific sourcing market, its costs, and actual suppliers is beyond the scope of this chapter. However, this chapter does introduce you to the three sourcing models (professional, vendor-led, or managed services) and the cost structures each model typically uses.

5. **Develop a sourcing strategy.** Are there a set of common practices, tools, beliefs, and documented procedures for resource managers to

follow that drive better pricing, selection, and oversight for vendor engagements?

6. **Negotiate with suppliers.** At this point, IT leadership determines who will be the best partner for the business, considering demand and supply situations as well as the need to minimize risk and costs. At a high-level, IT sourcing leadership determines the sourcing strategy (a strategic partnership, cosourced, vendor led, professional services, or a hybrid, depending on the services or project). Second, sourcing leadership defines the metrics for managing the contracts. In other words, what products, service levels, prices, geographical coverage, payment terms, and penalties define the strategic sourcing relationship?

7. **Track the results and restart the assessment.** Because many technical service centers deliver projects or services, a Center of Expertise (CoE) can solve the problem of tracking the progress and performance of the partnerships with vendors. To do this, the CoE establishes standards and processes to track results that manage strategic sourcing performance on an ongoing basis.

Unlike ITIL, a value-based strategic sourcing program cannot follow a standard libraries of steps and procedures that are shared across all companies. Instead, as strategic sourcing programs are put in place and practiced over time, organizations must modify and adapt internal processes to better meet the company's needs. The CoE can help the business manage its strategic partnerships so that these partnerships continue to support IT's value proposition.

Choosing a Strategic Sourcing Model

Outsourcing IT can take on many shapes and forms, each with unique challenges and benefits. This section introduces the three main strategic sourcing models: professional services, vendor-led services, and managed services. Table 8-1 outlines the high-level characteristics of each model, and the following sections discuss how each model works, when it's most useful, and other tips or issues to watch out for.

Table 8-1 Common Strategic Sourcing Models

Model	Services Provided	How It's Contracted
Professional services (also called *staff augmentation*)	Specific skill sets, such as project management, development, business analyst, BASIS, and so on	A purchase order defines a 1:1 relationship and a fixed rate card. Services are billed as time and materials (T&M).
Vendor-led services (also called *outside services*)	Specific deliverables with a fixed duration and scope, such as a new module or an entire project	A statement of work defines the duration or scope. Billing is aggregated across all resources and consolidated into one invoice.
Managed services	Day-to-day IT responsibilities and functions (Run the business)	A master service agreement (MSA) outlines the provider's fixed bid with a rider to handle exceptions or to create scale based on an agreed-upon tiered rate structure

Adding skill sets with professional services

In most cases, professional services provide temporary help to deliver a project or service, to provide a specific skill set, or to support a technical service center during times of increased demand. Here are examples of how businesses use professional services:

- When IT has skill shortage, such as support or project management, and cannot acquire this skill from other teams or departments
- When IT needs extra staff for an IT-funded project (staff augmentation).
- On occasion in a value-based IT culture, contractors backfill full-time employees' responsibilities on small projects or support operations so that full-time employees can work on larger projects (serving as functional leads to deliver the work normally outsourced to higher-paid consultants). Temporary professional services, when used this way, enable the full-time employees to work with users on key initiatives, keeping project accountability and intellectual property in-house and ensuring internal IT employees remain the face to the business.

> When using professional services, the operative word
> is *temporary,* because professional services often cost
> considerably more than internal employees.

To decrease overall IT costs, avoiding highly compensated contractors for long-term works stands to reason. However, professional services seem to stay on average, anywhere from 2-6 years, thereby increasing the overall cost of IT services and projects. For example, a IT project manager in Silicon Valley bills an average $136 per hour. Assuming that hiring an SAP project manager as an employee costs $189,000 (including base salary, bonus and benefits), the business can fill this long-term need with a new hire for $91 per hour. That $45 per hour means a contractor costs $93,000 more per year per headcount than a full-time employee. If the business has ten contractors working as IT project managers, the business is paying nearly $1 million dollars extra per year.

If the business has 100 of these contractors, that's an extra $10 million per year.

In companies that have shifted to contracting work for at least 75 percent of their project delivery, the cost of IT to the client increases. At some point, companies need to take a step back and ask some questions:

- How many professional services contractors are in the organization?
- How long have they been there?
- At what point does a company consider these services permanent instead of temporary?

Hiring a vendor to lead a temporary project

In some cases, a vendor-led engagement or partnership makes more sense than professional services. Vendor-led projects have a fixed outcome, where the service provided is expected to end and the vendor transitions responsibility to internal IT teams who manage the solution going forward. The following examples are common types of vendor-led projects:

- Delivering a new module — like master data management (MDM), customer relationship management (CRM), or advanced planner and optimizer (APO)
- Mapping and recommending a new solution for a critical business process like pricing, chargebacks, or contracts (specification and selection services)
- Planning and performing an upgrade for a critical business system

In the vendor-led model, the project is turned over to the supplier, and the organization manages only the contract. Vendor-led projects are typically sourced and structured as follows:

- To select a provider for vendor-led services, IT leadership starts with a request for proposal (RFP). After a vendor is selected, a statement of work (SOW) outlines key deliverables, fixed-cost rate cards, and measurements for project success. Engagements such as these may include adopting the vendor's software solution as part of the deliverables.

- Although the project is billed based on time and materials, payment also should be tied to key milestones in the SOW being met in order to ensure the relationship is mutually beneficial.

- The vendor is responsible for the delivery of the solution — unlike a cosourced model (discussed later in this chapter), where the vendor and internal IT have joint responsibility and accountability for the outcomes.

Using a vendor-led model has a number of upsides:

- Handing over a complete unit of work can increase project pipeline capacity for other initiatives. Further, internal resources are freed up, enabling them to provide oversight over more vendor-led projects being delivered at the same time, because the vendor is responsible for creating needed scale to hit project milestones.

- The vendor may introduce a new approach to project delivery or a different way of solving business problems not considered before.

- Because vendors bring expertise from multiple industries or similar customers, vendors can often implement new technologies faster than in-house staff.

However, the vendor-led model has its pitfalls, too. Before engaging with a vendor, business and IT leadership need to consider the following potential problems and, if they apply to the project, decide what steps can prevent major setbacks after the project is underway:

- When a vendor runs a project, companies find it challenging to accurately measure project health during the delivery cycle. Often, problems become apparent only as the production readiness or go-live milestones approach.

- When vendors work outside the company's project management office's processes, vendors can miss dependencies, such as upgrades, system freezes, user acceptance testing, or user training. These missed dependencies can then lead to missed deadlines, which have a ripple effect. The client, not the vendor, then must absorb the resulting incremental costs.

- Shifting accountability from internal IT to a vendor can insulate IT leadership from a project's actual outcomes. As a result, internal IT is inadequately engaged in project oversight, and after the vendor rolls off the project, internal IT is unprepared to assume responsibility for the project's outcomes or support.

- When the ERP environment is highly customized, the vendor may take several weeks or even months to reverse-engineer the systems and become proficient in a complex IT landscape. After the vendor discovers what the company is actually doing in the systems, the project scope may need to expand or be redesigned.

- A vendor's unique methodology can lead to problems passing internal code reviews and QA standards, causing delays.

In addition, without an internal technical lead or project manager, vendors may be unable to effectively acquire services or support from technical service centers or internal shared services, causing delays to the project and additional costs. The biggest risk is that vendors do not have the relationships needed to effectively work with the business partners and understand their processes, leading to missed requirements or a design that needs to be revisited during user acceptance testing. By not understanding the internal business processes or politics, vendors must take all information provided at face value on how work is performed. Business partners can take advantage of the vendor's naïveté to increase scope or leave out critical information, and vendors are unable to challenge these requirements.

The key success factor for vendor-led engagements is keeping process oversight in-house to effectively manage projects through the delivery lifecycle.

Oversight includes providing consistent reporting on the project's health, status, risks, issues, and escalations. To ensure this, the project manager (PM) roles *should be filled internally* by someone knowledgeable about the business processes and application software being delivered. The PM serves as the gatekeeper between the vendor, leadership, business, technical service centers, and the internal applications team.

In some companies, senior PMs are former business analysts and have gone through at least one or two lifecycle implementations of the application technology. If no qualified internal PMs can manage the project, the PM should be sourced from a different vendor than the one being used for delivery of the project to prevent a conflict of interest, thereby ensuring the PM manages changes in scope for the good of the project and not for the vendor's financial gain.

Vendor-led projects also require some additional full-time employees to be embedded in the project. These employees work with the PM and the vendor to facilitate collaboration across technical service centers, such as BASIS, security, QA, and infrastructure. Also, embedding full-time employees helps keep intellectual property in-house, reducing the risks after the project is complete and internal IT begins supporting the new or upgraded technology. Without embedded full-time employees, support isn't a key consideration in designing, blueprinting, and building the solution, and the vendor likely won't discuss support until the initiative enters the project readiness phase.

Outsourcing day-to-day IT work to a managed service provider

As discussed in earlier chapters, sometimes companies want to turn over the responsibility for day-to-day projects, operations, and/or support to a managed service vendor. Companies do this for a number of reasons, and Figure 8-1 illustrates the top four reasons, based on a number of studies.

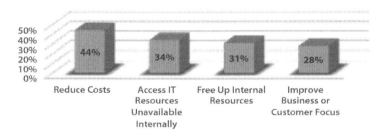

Figure 8-1

When good quantitative data is available to measure service performance, the managed service model can be ideal for certain IT-run processes or support, such as system monitoring, help desk, testing and test automation, development, resetting passwords, and tier-one support. In the managed service model, the vendor is responsible for hiring, on-boarding, training, and off-boarding its employees. The vendor's competency in the company's IT landscape improves over time, and its employees leverage a knowledge base system that increases the quality of support-related services. Outsourcing can include an entire service area (like support and help desk) or specific roles (like development, security, BASIS, or testing).

To reduce IT costs, managed services blend off-shore or near-shore employees with on-shore employees. When compiling a managed service agreement, companies need to consider the following factors and how each provider's blend of off-, near-, and on-shore employees might impact the company's operations and strategy:

- **Communications:** IT communicates with its customers based on the value proposition IT offers different groups of customers. The MSA needs to include the strategy to ensure the appropriate level of communication with the customer.

- **Attrition rate:** The company assumes more risk when a vendor has high attrition rates for key resources, such as when junior people gain proficiency and look for more lucrative jobs.

- **Cultural compatibility:** This includes business culture

- **Time zones:** If collaboration or access to business partners and/or other IT shared services is critical, a near-shore solution might be ideal.

- **Billing rates:** The blended rate versus the offshore rate is key to managing the cost of managed services. For example, consider scenarios like if the managed service provider increases the on-shore footprint, such as during an upgrade, how competitive is this new blended rate? Be careful not to commit to one vendor for all services like disaster recovery and upgrades with an assumption these tasks can be done at the offshore cost.

- **Skill sets and resource management:** What is the vendor's pool of IT expertise for the applications and/or services to support? Companies need to consider the vendor's reputation as well as how the vendor's employees are rotated to other accounts or customers.

- **Political environment:** As mentioned earlier, the number of countries hosting outsourcing has nearly doubled in the last decade. Each comes with political and economic risks.

- **Infrastructure:** What tools does the vendor bring to drive efficiencies? What products must the organization license and maintain?

When choosing a managed service provider, companies also need to consider the following:

- **What delivery methodology (SDLC, Waterfall, ASAP, Agile, and so on) the provider uses:** Some delivery methods (like ITIL) work better with offshore than others (SDLC).

- **How the vendor manages the actual transition:** For example, ask how the vendor gathers system information and standard operating procedures and documents critical business processes into a knowledge center. In some cases, internal employees who are let go are offered a chance to be re-badged as a member of the outsourcing firm to help with knowledge transfer and provide services for an agreed-upon amount of time.

In the managed services model, companies control their costs by locking into a master service agreement (MSA) for three to five years. The managed services model requires the most metrics for contract oversight, administration, and change management, when compared with other models. Thus, when assessing managed service providers, companies need to be thoughtful about how cost savings are quantified. For example, when outsourcing development, incremental costs are incurred when business analysts and on-site coordinators spend additional time to provide more detailed documentation to offshore resources. Passing a functional and technical specification nightly to the off-shore teams may have qualitative consequences, such as reducing innovation or causing delays. In this model, off-shore teams don't have the same opportunity as colocated teams to exchange ideas or to ask for clarification of technical requirements without losing a 24-hour cycle.

Although outsourcing and off-shore can reduce costs for work that's predictive and scripted, other factors need to be considered for roles like development and business or functional analysis. Companies must find a way to compare when hourly savings using off-shore labor is lost on tasks requiring greater collaboration across teams and with the customer.

Managed services are not ideal to support project delivery, new technology, or new module implementation. Further, this model does not work well for requesting on-site temporary professional services, because the rates for T&M professional services are often higher for any work outside scope of the MSA than using other sourcing strategies.

Choosing the Right Sourcing Strategy

After business and IT leadership decide what sourcing model to use, the IT leadership needs to define internal IT's relationship with its strategic sourcing partners. Temporary workers hired under the professional services model are typically individuals integrated with internal IT teams to provide a specific skill set. However, when vendor-led projects or managed service providers become part of the IT landscape, defining the vendor's relationship with internal IT becomes more complex.

As mentioned in the preceding sections, with a value-based IT strategy, IT can't simply hand off work to vendors. To ensure project success, manage costs, and ensure knowledge transfer after vendors complete temporary projects, companies need some full-time employees to help manage the relationship with the vendor. Also, SOWs and MSAs need to be constructed to create mutually beneficial relationships for the business and the vendor.

This section focuses on the overall strategy that guides how employees are integrated into outsourced projects or services: a cosource strategy or a strategic partnership. You also learn at a high-level how these relationships are defined in contracts and other agreements. (A strategic sourcing Center of Expertise, discussed later in this chapter, also helps ensure that SOWs, MSAs, and other vendor agreements lay a good foundation for vendor relationships.)

For each outsourcing relationship, IT leadership needs to consider what vendor-relationship strategy is the right fit based on existing capacity and the project's size and complexity.

Integrating strategic sourcing partners with the IT team (Cosource strategy)

A cosource strategy, in which the vendor is treated like an extension of the IT team, works well for temporary engagements, such as implementing a new technology or module.

In a cosource strategy, vendors are hired specifically for the innovation, industry knowledge, and experience they bring. However, cosourcing is also a model of shared responsibility, where in-house employees and vendors collaborate as follows:

- Senior internal resources are assigned for business analyst, functional, and project management to provide oversight of vendor deliverables.

- To improve outcomes, vendors help manage any change in the scope and the timelines.

- To reduce delays and rework, employees help the vendor understand complex business processes and current operational constraints in the IT landscape.

- Both parties establish and agree to value-based criteria versus profit for outcomes.

- Reduce focus on contract oversight by embedding internal resources in the project and, in some cases, having internal resources lead the initiatives in-house.

In other words, working together with vendors allows internal employees to focus on value-based outcomes, such as quality, usability, and solution support instead of spending their time on the oversight of vendor-led deliverables and contract administration.

In a cosource model, tribal knowledge is leveraged to gain better alignment and remove roadblocks more quickly. Internal technical leads provide an integration layer across enterprise IT shared services and other technical server centers to increase speed to market. In this way, embedded employees help companies to leverage higher-cost vendor resources for their innovation and their emerging technologies skills while ensuring intellectual property remains in-house.

To define the business's relationship with the vendor as a cosource relationship, the following contracts and documents are typically used:

- **SOW:** The SOW includes rules of engagement that define how the partnership works. The SOW also outlines the costs, which are typically higher than costs in a strategic partnership. SOWs can be authored to accommodate changes in scope as time plus materials with target cost ceilings that trigger contract modifications.
- **RACI matrix:** RACI stands for Responsible, Accountable, Informed, and Consulted. To ensure success, this matrix is developed in partnership with the vendor to prevent the lines being blurred during project delivery.
- **Communication matrix:** This matrix defines how project health and escalating issues are reported to IT leadership and how to manage information flowing between the IT teams, IT leadership, and the business partners they serve.

Creating a strategic partnership with a managed service provider

In a strategic partnership, IT leverages the advantages of using a single provider's expertise, processes, and tools for a fixed and predictable cost that is less than internal headcount but more than outsourcing through a typical managed services contract.

A strategic partnership can be ideal for certain ERP run processes or support (such as monitoring, help desk, QA testing, test automation, development, resetting passwords, or tier-one support). A strategic partnership can also be used to create capacity for predictable or scripted build processes (projects), such as Oracle and ERP upgrades, system validation, and service pack updates. With the right alignment of operations and project development resources into a single delivery resource pool (as discussed in Chapter 7), strategic partnerships scale teams to provide skill sets for projects such as development, ETL, security, and other technical deliverables that can be captured in a technical specification and given to off-shore workers.

In some cases, companies can also hire professional services from a managed service provider normally sourced using staff augmentation. The key is agree to rate cards that mitigate the aforementioned high charges for professional services not accounted for in the MSA. Then, IT can systematically staff-augment teams with a trusted partner for roles such as project managers or developers if additional sets of hands are needed temporarily. However, the risk is that using one vendor for staffing reduces the pool to find on-site resources in a short time.

However, a strategic partnerships may not be the best choice when developing or supporting new technologies or for sizing new projects, creating proposals or blueprints, or designing a new solution.

In a strategic partnership, the company and the vendor collaborate as follows:

- IT leadership architects the onshore/offshore blend based on what the business is willing to spend and the risks it's willing to take. The vendor does not retain control of all staffing decisions or levels because the business relationship is not a fixed bid. However, the IT team doesn't interview individual resources, and the actual costs for offshore versus onshore delivery aren't completely transparent.
- The vendor manages on-boarding, training, and off-boarding.
- The vendor and client jointly develop development standards and processes that the service provider will follow.
- The vendor develops a knowledge base to increase quality and speed-to-market.

Benefits of a strategic partnership include the following:

- When IT leadership is planning and sizing the department for upcoming projects or services, costs are predictable due to fixed time and materials rates.
- Onshore/offshore blended rates are leveraged to reduce costs.
- The vendor's competency with the IT landscape improves over time.

The contracts and metrics that define a strategic partnership are similar to those for a managed service offering but not volume based (like number of tickets) but rather:

- Billing is based on time and materials.
- A SOW and/or MSA is established with fixed rates for skill sets.
- The IT team provides the vendor with forecasts for the needed scale at a predetermined interval.
- The vendor tracks the time spent on the project using a workforce-management system, enabling accurate billing of hours by task.

Matching the sourcing strategy to IT's overall goals

Here are some overall considerations to keep in mind when selecting a strategic sourcing model and strategy for project delivery:

- **Costs versus quality:** Strategic partnerships offer the best outcomes, controls, and costs through negotiating fixed rates that stay in effect no matter how many projects are worked on or what incremental capacity is required. Although the actual rates in a strategic partnership are higher than in a traditional managed services model, the true costs are more predictable. Long-term partnerships provide continuity not found in temporary professional services vendors.

- **Flexibility and scalability:** Professional services vendors respond most quickly to changes in staffing levels. In contrast, vendor-led projects with a specific SOW require more time to staff and more administrative overhead. Managed services providers can add capacity off-shore, but providing on-site resources is more difficult.

- **Speed to market:** Teams that are insourced and staff augmented with professional services can deliver any solution faster than teams using another sourcing strategy because internal employees know the IT landscape, the business processes, and the business partners. In the insourced model, contractors are embedded on-site with internal IT employees. Insourced teams leverage relationships with internal IT to remove roadblocks. When the business is willing to pay for speed and quality, using professional services to ramp up and down is ideal.

- **Competency:** If you can control the competency of teams, you can predict outcomes. For projects, professional services integrated with the IT team following an insource or cosource strategy results in less rework, fewer issues, and fewer defects post-go-live while providing a faster transition to support.

- **Emerging technologies:** Hiring professional services vendors or establishing vendor agreements with a SOW results in higher success for emerging technologies than managed services or strategic partnerships.

Establishing a Center of Expertise (CoE) for Strategic Sourcing

Companies moving toward external vendors to provide scale, reduce costs, and increase throughput will require a new competency to in order to effectively manage costs, evaluate vendor performance, and ensure predictable outcomes.

Keep in mind, the sourcing philosophy or approach for each engagement may look slightly different depending on the SOW or MSA, and a one-size-fits-all sourcing strategy may not be ideal for every engagement. For example, should the vendor always follow internal standard SDLC, ITIL, ITSM, Agile or scrum methodologies? The answer really depends on the engagement type for a couple of reasons. In the managed service and vendor-led models, the vendor should have some autonomy in how it delivers the products and services because the vendor is liable for the outcomes. The vendor would prefer to fail on its own terms versus due to internal challenges the organization has with its own inefficient SDLC or ITSM methodologies.

With a strategic sourcing Center of Expertise (CoE), IT has the skills it needs to establish standard operating procedures for strategic sourcing, while still recognizing the subtle differences in the engagement types. The CoE can craft SOPs that are flexible and that the vendor and the internal employees can understand. More importantly, when the processes are adopted and followed, this ensures repeatable and predictable outcomes.

Although forming an entire division or strategic sourcing department may not be necessary, a Center of Expertise (CoE) model can provide a framework and philosophy that enables the organization to make strategic sourcing decisions quickly by removing uncertainty and doubt.

When IT organizations analyze the cost of a strategic sourcing program and the return on investment for a specific strategy or vendor, IT organizations must factor in the cost of a strategic sourcing program for managing the vendor and providing oversight.

The following sections explain some of the CoE's key responsibilities and outline a framework for adding a CoE to the IT landscape.

Communicating processes to employees and vendors

The CoE ensures that employees and vendors see the connection between the logic of the delivery processes and the expected results. For example, say internal project managers are responsible and accountable for project scope. In contracts that define the vendor relationship, the CoE ensures that the project has a clearly defined scope and change-control processes. Moreover, when project schedules are adjusted or costs increase, the CoE includes workflow and sign-offs from the business that protect both the vendor and the IT organization.

The CoE defines these processes up-front to both the project team members and business partners during the project kick-off. By laying this groundwork, the CoE prevents project resources from making promises that increase the vendor's revenue but are bad for the PMO.

Establishing and tracking service-level agreements

With an increasing dependency on outside, professional, and managed services, IT organizations need a new discipline for managing vendor engagements. A CoE philosophy and framework provides the code of conduct for everyone to follow that is simple and easy to understand, thereby ensuring little or no hesitation on how to address questions or problems as they arise. To do this, the CoE establishes and tracks service level agreements (SLAs) between the vendor and client.

An SLA includes the following:

- **Processes:** The SLA calls out processes that govern all deliverables, such as design, Business Blue Prints (BPPs), functional specs, unit test plans (UTPs), and so on. The SLA should also outline how the client's functional or technical leads approve workflow before any system transports are moved through the environment.

- **Metrics for tracking:** The CoE workflow tracks what dates deliverables are turned over for review and the time elapsed for internal review or rejection. Metrics are very important. For example, capturing rejections and comments on deliverables enables the organization to mine this information as part of the root cause analysis process to assess skill set gaps for the vendors. Furthermore, sign offs at key gates protects the vendor and internal IT for post go-live usability claims. Establishing good SOPs, workflow, and training reduces risks and enables the CoE to measure a vendor's performance and competence in real time. When the CoE has the right metrics for tracking, the CoE can recommend staffing changes to be made quickly when needed due to skill set gaps.

Driving accountability

Remember, creating a CoE drives more accountability for the vendor, internal IT, and the business partners alike. When vendors and employees understand what they are measured on, they do not waste time finger pointing or having turf wars on who's responsible for the delays because quantitative data collected during workflow cannot be disputed.

For example, if your specification was due on Friday the 19th, you delivered it a week later, and there were no agreed-upon changes to the project plan, then you missed your deliverables. End of discussion. If this is a pattern, then end of assignment for the resource.

Furthermore, this quantitative data and workflow documentation can be used to recover costs or justify adjustments to the vendor invoices as needed. This is why the CoE must establish and track SLAs through agreed-upon metrics between the vendor and internal key resources. If the metrics are not accurate or relevant, they will not be adopted or useful for contract oversight. The goal is to prevent missed commitments that result in a ripple effect and impact the project's timeline and costs.

Developing a CoE framework

Although each organization is different, the following are some considerations to make when developing a strategic sourcing CoE framework:

To begin, lay the groundwork for success by doing the following:

- Identify your CoE build/run process for self-assessments. Determine what's in scope for the following:
  — Types of projects (build processes)
  — Support and operations (run processes)
- Create a CoE document management system (DMS) and strategy and define the following:
  — Document storage structure
  — Workflow and approvals
- Develop a change-control approval workflow for vendor development. Make sure the workflow addresses the following questions:
  — What approvals and reporting will be in place to measure the vendor's success?
  — What tools will be used to capture and report on defects?
- Establish how vendors will be evaluated on a regular basis.

In addition to the building blocks, each organization needs to define the frequency and criteria for its vendor evaluations. Monitoring the vendors must be woven into the fabric of daily life for the IT organization through the following internal assessments and reporting:

- **CoE run/build process self-assessments:** These are weekly team self-assessments by project across peer groups. Conduct these assessments when a gap occurs between skill sets and workmanship or when either internal IT or the vendor doesn't follow the prescribed approach.
- **CoE document management system workflow:** Workflow reporting can drive different behaviors by communicating what SLA metrics vendors or internal employees completed or missed.
- **Change-management reports:** These reports include code and configuration reviews and QA test results. The purpose of these reports is to provide transparency regarding technical gaps or delays caused by noncompliance. These gaps are identified using workflow to capture the following:
  — Deliverables rejected in unit test or QA
  — Missing or substandard functional specifications or UTPs
  — Missed dates for delivering on commitments
- **Vendor scorecards:** These scorecards gather feedback from leadership and stakeholders to provide the vendor and internal IT feedback on the vendor's performance. Scorecards also validate weekly and monthly success in performing the self-assessments.

Creating the needed templates and documentation

As a starting point, organizations develop standard templates and identify when those templates apply to a project or IT services. Depending of the language of the SOW or master service agreement, vendors may use their own templates in some cases, but first, IT leads should review and approve vendor templates to ensure they meet internal IT audit criteria.

In addition, the CoE publishes workflow diagrams and SOPs, and all resources acknowledge they've reviewed this documentation via an electronic tracking system. A learning management system (LMS) can be used track who has received and reviewed updated documentation. This tracking removes any doubt that internal processes and standards have been cascaded to the vendor resources.

The workflow and SOP documentation that the CoE needs to provide includes, but is not limited to, the following:

- Onboarding and training materials for both internal and external resources

- A document management strategy and knowledge base
- Change management processes that outline how code moves through the environments and approvals
- Testing and quality-control strategies, including performance testing best practices
- Governance for proof of concept (POC), blueprint and design reviews, specifications and UTPs, code reviews, configuration reviews, and the Test Center of Excellence if it exists
- Well-defined system development lifecycle processes for each engagement type
- Instructions on engaging shared services or internal technical service centers (TSCs)
- Workforce-, capacity-, and demand-management responsibilities (including timekeeping)
- Escalation processes
- A communication matrix that explains who engages who at what levels
- Contract oversight and administration roles, responsibilities, and procedures for contract modifications or requests for accord and satisfaction from the vendors.

Case Study: My Strategic Sourcing Journey and *The Wizard of Oz*

In this section, I share a case study that illustrates how all the elements of strategic sourcing fit together — including choosing the right blend of professional, vendor-led, and managed services; choosing the right vendor and strategy; and setting up a CoE.

I initially presented this case study at the 2011 SAPinsider *Outsourcing in Your SAP Environment* conference in Las Vegas, NV, under the title "A behind-the-scenes look at a strategic sourcing strategy and outsourcing experiences in a Fortune 500 company." The abstract highlighted the shifting landscape around professional, outside, and managed services driving the need for strategic sourcing to be treated as a competency center. I chose to use a familiar motif to illustrate the case study — *The Wizard of Oz.*

How outsourcing swept me into Oz

When it came to outsourcing, I couldn't help but feel like Dorothy after the strategic sourcing tornado blew through my organization. I was lost in a strange land searching for the Emerald City to ask the Great Wizard to help me find my way home. As I began my journey down the yellow brick road of vendor solutions, like Dorothy, I first encountered the Wicked Witch of the East (outsourcing pitfalls):

- Onboarding and orientation challenges for vendors
- Lack of compliance with internal standards and processes
- Vaporware (promised system functionality or services that do not come to fruition)
- Skill set gaps among the vendor's IT team
- Rework on standard deliverables, such as blueprint, BPML, business process procedures (BPPs), functional specifications, unit test plans, and so on

As I continued on my way, I realized I needed more knowledge about this new sourcing dilemma. Like the Scarecrow, I was convinced if I only had a brain I could figure how improve the outcomes for outside services contracts (that is, vendor-led services). So I decided to perform an assessment to ponder the following questions:

- What worked well in the past?
- What is working today?
- What is not working?
- How can better measurements and controls be established to ensure predictable outcomes?

During the assessment, I learned firsthand how both outside services and offshore outsourcing was having a negative impact on employees, and that the transition to vendor-led services was an emotional and sensitive topic. In some cases, outsourcing had replaced long-term employee jobs with lower-cost laborers. In others, outside services were being employed to deliver solutions when internal employees were better suited to perform the work.

I believed the organization had to find a heart (like the Tin Man) to address the growing employee disillusionment, frustration, and apathy from the increased dependency on vendors and ongoing reduction in full-time employees. There was no doubt that outsourcing was destabilizing internal employees and impacting productivity. I knew more than ever I needed to find the Emerald City and the Wizard if I were to restore the trust of the workforce.

I began to gather more information around our strategic sourcing dilemma. After all problems were cataloged, I realized that to improve vendor outcomes, many changes across IT teams and the organization were needed. Like the Cowardly Lion, I would need to find the courage in a politically charged environment to create increased accountability around the following:

- Vendor delivery teams (outside services and professional services contractors)
- Internal technical delivery leads (functional analysts and PMs)
- Internal technical service centers
- Business partners and stakeholders

Luckily, I received a visit from Glenda, the Good Witch of the North (actually my colleagues in user sustainment who gave me the idea). She asked, "Are you having trouble with getting the vendor outcomes you seek?" Glenda waved her wand and a blueprint for a strategic sourcing Center of Expertise (CoE) appeared. With Glenda's help, I began to build out a CoE framework with clear objectives, build processes, and measurements.

However, although I designed a CoE framework and got buy-in from management, project teams, vendors, business partners and TSCs, the Wicked Witch and Flying Monkeys returned, and I was not out of the woods yet. In-flight projects and strategic vendor relationships (SOWs) were already established and not aligned with the best practices in the new CoE. This meant the new strategy needed to be launched in concert with delivering on existing commitments and honoring old statements of work.

Arriving at the Emerald City

When I finally arrived at the Emerald City, I now had the needed governance, controls, and measurements in place to manage the vendors. But something was still not right, and I realized the Wizard of Oz continued to pull levers behind the curtain that I could not see or control. To address this, I needed to work with the executive leadership team to ensure the approach considered IT goals and priorities (scorecards) for the year.

This would prevent changes in organizational priorities from decreasing the company's chance for success with vendor-led solutions. For example, if a team that was supporting a key initiative or launching a new delivery methodology were downsized, the loss of this team would impact project dependencies on other teams.

Like the Wizard of Oz, this story had a happy ending because, despite all the obstacles, establishing a strategic sourcing competency center (CoE) proved to be the right solution for creating repeatable processes that ensure predictable outcomes. The CoE provided measurements that both vendors and internal employees trusted. This in turn provided the needed exposure mechanisms to drive increased accountability, resulting in higher quality, less rework, and higher customer satisfaction.

Chapter Summary

When choosing the strategic sourcing approach, each organization needs to consider its customers' value proposition, customer relationship type, financial goals, risk aversion, and desire to promote organizational health. Each model (professional services, vendor-led, or managed services) may make sense at different times in an IT organization's maturity, depending on financial constraints.

The common thread around a successful strategic sourcing strategy is that the client (internal IT), not the vendor, takes responsibility for oversight and outcomes. Accountability must remain within the IT organization for all operations, projects, and programs. Put simply, companies can no longer afford to hand over their application software destiny to vendors. Instead, they must leverage vendors in ways that complement the organization's strengths versus building an IT organization heavily dependent on outside services.

An organization can increase its odds of success by applying these strategic sourcing best practices:

- Create a vendor management competency center or (CoE) for developing RFPs, SOWs, and MSAs and defining the SDLC and governance.
- Use vendors to provide expertise where appropriate to lower costs and create scale while developing a long-term plan to correct the lack of this expertise in the organization.
- Structure vendor engagements so that metrics cannot misrepresented and to drive accountability and the right behaviors from the vendor resources
- Recognize the value proposition of integrating your full-time employees with vendors to ensure intellectual property is kept in-house, thereby creating self-reliance for future development.
- Ensure the vendor's success through a shared success model, where internal IT and business partners alike follow through on their commitments.

The ability to drive high performance hinges on building processes and measurements that both the employee and vendors can trust. Furthermore, employees should be able to see the connection between the strategy, logic, and the results. Creating a CoE for vendor management drives these benefits:

- Standardizes processes and policy across delivery teams

- Develops key success criteria and measurements
- Removes doubt and uncertainty about culture and processes
- Provides more innovation and faster decision making
- Stabilizes the population under pressure or during times of significant change
- Creates better alignment (internal IT, TSCs, business partners, and vendor)
- Provides repeatable vendor-delivery standards and procedures to ensure predictable outcomes
- Ensures better early life support (ELS), warranty, and knowledge transfer (KT) standards for supportability
- Provides a feedback loop to improve future RFPs and SOWs

Successful organizations create program oversight and make needed investments to include internal resources when engaging vendors for large-scale implementations or support agreements. However, it is not just the oversight that needs consideration; rather it is the value-based mindset of treating the vendor like a partner, not just the lowest-cost commodity to get the cheapest solution. When the vendor and client cultures share responsibility and accountability, outcomes improve. A "we" mentality reduces friction and improves productivity.

> Strategic sourcing requires a different discipline than insourcing to provide the needed governance over a vendor delivery model. As dependency on vendors increases, project change-control processes need to adapt to call out key deliverables, timelines, and remediation processes in order to hold vendors accountable for outcomes.

CHAPTER 9

FIFTH PROTOCOL: THE IT BRAND

A well-crafted brand is iconic and builds consumers' trust in the brand's products and services. Customers associate brands such as Starbucks, Nike, and Mercedes, with an experience, whether real or perceived. Like brands that are a household name, IT organizations must manage their brand effectively by being thoughtful about their communications, products, and services.

Customers don't have to buy a Mercedes — or even a Honda — to commute from one location to another. They choose to — in part because those customers want the quality, reputation, and service history for which the brand is known. In the same spirit, rather than competing on price alone, a value-based IT organization finds a middle ground between value and cost by providing high-quality services at a competitive price. After IT customers experience the quality of this offering, they're unlikely to sacrifice service levels for lower costs.

To be clear, developing the IT brand isn't about naming the IT organization, creating a logo, or crafting new templates for everyone to use. Rather, an internal IT brand sets customer's expectations regarding the value proposition of IT products and services and ensures IT's actual outcomes follow through on that value proposition. Managing the IT brand has three key components:

- Connecting the IT brand to the outcomes IT delivers in the minds of its customers, including internal users and business partners
- Defining common practices that IT teams follow in order to support the brand

- Helping individuals understand and develop their personal brand as a way of developing their careers and their contribution to the IT organization

This chapter explains the rewards of developing an IT brand (and the risks of going without one), as well as how to create a framework that clarifies the ways employees can create, support, and define the brand in their day-to-day work and interactions with IT customers.

What Are the Benefits of an IT Brand?

One common denominator among failed ERP implementations, failed IT projects, and poor IT operational performance is lack of alignment with the customer. That is, the relationship between IT and its customers becomes adversarial in one or more of the following ways:

- IT customers do not differentiate between poor service levels or poor performance from one team and the rest of IT. Failure in support or on any one project can carry over into other engagements with the customers of IT for other service areas.

- IT customers might not fully commit to the technology roadmap or perceive an IT-sponsored project as an inconvenience because IT hasn't effectively communicated how the project will ultimately benefit them and the company as a whole.

- IT doesn't provide the necessary staffing, skills, and support infrastructure to help IT customers transition from the old system to the new one.

- IT's profit-based objectives for the services are not aligned with the promised value proposition.

These factors create friction between IT and its customers, which hurts the forward momentum of an initiative or project. Left unchecked, this friction results in conflict that further reduces trust and successful customer engagement. This friction also seeds fear of failure, doubt of competency, and frustration that in turn, leads to reduced productivity and further tarnishes the internal IT brand. Even after friction is removed, collateral damage to IT's reputation can continue to reduce efficiency when the trust has been breached.

When the IT brand is properly managed, IT is proactive about how IT customers perceive the value they provide. In other words, the problem with IT transformations is not always what IT does, but rather how the expectations of the services or solutions are managed. Further, are the outcomes aligned with the promise?

For example, system availability can be at 99.9 percent and incident tickets at an all-time low, and yet the day-to-day customer experience may put IT and its clients in an adversarial position. In contrast, when the IT brand is properly managed, projects can experience bumps in the road, such as missed deadlines, system outages, and so on, but with the right communications and customer service, customers still identify IT as being customer-service oriented and providing high-quality work. Managing the people factor is the key to implementing the project successfully, ensuring adoption of solutions, and maximizing the return on investment (ROI) for IT technology and employee assets.

Effective IT branding results in higher levels of internal collaboration, performance, and adoption of solutions, because the IT brand gives both employees and customers reasons to have positive experiences, beliefs, and attitudes about IT services and solutions.

Developing the IT Brand among Users and Business Partners

To create alignment and prevent or remove friction, IT leadership needs to foster trust with the workforce and customers alike by communicating IT's value proposition and tying actions to that value proposition.

Creating alignment starts by developing a clear IT business model to define how IT brings value to its customers. In other words, IT and its customers need to agree on what services or projects are possible given the budget and human and physical assets. Working from that knowledge, IT leadership can develop a strategy to communicate the value proposition to the IT teams and clients alike. For example, if the IT brand is to provide the low-cost, no-frills IT services, then the messaging should convey this brand promise, instead of advertising quality, speed to market, or customer service.

When IT leadership develops the IT brand, the goal is to ensure that IT customers and workers see a connection between the IT brand and the outcomes being delivered.

Much of the work done in the First through Fourth Protocols helps to clarify what IT's value proposition is. As explained in earlier chapters, determining the value proposition — and thus defining the IT brand — works best when organizations approach users, customers, and business partners with a shared-success model to prevent the client from feeling alienated or disenfranchised. The decision about whether to automate or personalize each service that IT offers should be made collaboratively with IT teams and clients — not by management or consultants focused on architecting cost-savings strategies. There are many approaches when developing the business model for client engagement: personal assistance, dedicated personal assistance, self-service, automated services, co-creation, and user and technical communities. For each service or capability area, IT management should make sure the approach is aligned with client expectations. These decisions ultimately drive the IT brand.

After IT leadership understands what the IT brand is, they can develop the messaging, which includes the following:

- **The format:** Use headings that will grab the audience's attention, graphics that present some information visually, and language that non-IT people can understand.

- **The medium:** You might use emails, newsletters, or blog posts about upcoming or ongoing IT projects. Where you choose to communicate really depends on how information flows in the organization. For example, if IT customers access a home page or portal regularly to run reports, request routine services, or see dashboards, then this home page or portal might be more effective than a newsletter. The goal is to create transparency for the IT roadmap and keep the customers informed by sharing information wherever IT customers already communicate.

- **The measurements:** After IT leadership knows how it will communicate with users, make a plan to measure how effective communications are. Use analytics to track the number of readers against the size of your target audience and adjust the strategy to increase the followers.

Although I stated earlier that developing an brand isn't about a logo or templates, IT leadership may nevertheless use common branding elements to convey IT's value proposition and help customers recall and recognize the IT brand. Because IT is often decentralized, logos can help customer quickly identify when they are in the right place to ask for assistance. If you support SAP, Informatica, SalesForce.com, Workday, and so on, feathering this into the branding can help reduce confusion about the services provided.

These branding elements also help that customers know which of their needs the brand can satisfy. Here are some examples of common branding elements and examples of how IT leadership might incorporate them into the messaging for the IT brand:

- **Name:** A name identifies a company, product, service, or concept. Naming helps customers determine whether they're in the right place. From the customer's perspective, IT includes everything from computers, to telecom, networks, databases, applications, and portals. Yet in IT, these often fall under completely different departments. Providing a clear description of the technical service center, department, and global IT service areas helps remove confusion.

- **Logo:** A logo is an image associated with a brand, like Nike's swoosh symbol or the circular logo on a BMW. Like the name, each area may provide distinct services and an icon can serve to help customers create the association visually.

- **Colors:** Tiffany blue is recognizable globally. An IT organization doesn't need to bring in Pantone to develop and copyright a color for its ERP implementation, but might use colors to develop an emotional response to the brand. Google uses crisp upper/lowercase lettering with playful colors which aligns with its culture. What is the culture of your IT department, and what emotional response do you want your customer to have?

- **Tagline or catchphrase:** A tagline provides a little more information about a brand's promise. At the company Kaiser Permanente, the tagline is "Where care and coverage come together." Internally, another company's warehouse distribution business for cancer drugs used the tagline, "It's a patient, not a package." This tagline supported the desired customer experience and value proposition by emphasizing the importance of delivering all orders with care and operational efficiency.

From a customer's viewpoint, the IT experience is determined not by a single outcome but by the sum of all points of contact with the IT organization. In other words, the brand is symbolic, created within the minds of people, and includes all the information about past experiences and future expectations associated with a product or service. The goal of any IT brand element is to align expectations around the brand experience and create an impression that a brand has certain qualities or characteristics that make it special or unique.

After IT leadership defines the brand, they can begin using the brand to orient IT customers and workers to IT's value proposition. IT can also begin collecting information about the positive or negative sentiment towards the brand. When properly architected, a brand can convey a level of quality or other characteristic (the brand promise), thereby enabling services to command higher prices.

Although a brand is defined as an intangible asset, it can be the most valuable asset in the business cost structure. Like companies that manage their brands carefully to create shareholder value, IT leaders must focus on long-term stewardship of the IT brand by delivering on the promises of value in order to champion future investments from IT customers and justify higher costs. In this way, the IT brand becomes the cornerstone for managing the business partner engagement and client relationships.

Defining IT Practices That Support the IT Brand

To increase alignment, key resources need clarity around goals, deliverables, operational procedures, accountability, and expectations. Developing an IT brand includes creating a framework of values, shared language, and expected behaviors for all IT key resources that enable them to manage, measure, and improve the value proposition of IT. Whereas the First through Fourth Protocols develop the strategy, the IT employee–focused component of the IT brand lays the foundation to ensure that strategic processes are followed consistently to create trust with clients.

For IT employees and resources, an internal brand creates a sense of purpose as well as a strong emotional tie to fulfilling the value proposition. As explained in the following sections, the internal brand can be both global for IT and also unique or distinct to behaviors for each technical service center.

Outlining global practices

Everyone in IT needs to engage customers using the same playbook. Some improvement areas for the IT brand might require building new in-house skill sets to improve service levels, or adopting best practices like application performance monitoring (APM) to proactively identify system issues before users see them. However, other opportunities just require more transparency when creating the IT strategy.

For example, to remove friction and increase project success, organizations can define and adopt a common set of practices that are relevant for all IT service areas and tied to the value proposition, such as the following:

- Proactively manage the technology/business relationship.
- Integrate business strategies that include technology and services into strategic planning.

- Understand IT's role in the multiyear roadmap for the overall business strategy.
- Ensure the skill sets and processes are in place to support the program.
- Establish global prioritization and a transparent planning process.
- Create increased business accountability for the adoption of IT solutions.

The last two warrant additional context because they are broad in nature and at a glance, do not seem to relate to proceeding protocols. However, they are important factors for managing customers' expectations:

- **Global prioritization:** Most IT organizations work with limited OPEX budgets that cannot satisfy all of customers' demands and in some cases IT's own initiatives. To help customers and IT jointly prioritize how the limited dollars are spent each year, the technology roadmap needs to be built in concert with the business IT roadmap. More importantly, aligning these two roadmaps can encourage IT customers to champion more IT funding if the pool of dollars cannot satisfy the business objectives.
- **Business accountability:** Just as IT organizations take risks when they turn over their IT destinies to external vendors, IT customers take risks when they hand over the reins of their business solutions to internal IT organizations and take no accountability for the outcomes. IT and its customers need to share the same success model and accountability for outcomes.

Not everything about managing the brand is difficult. Often it's about creating an experience for the customer that is predictable and repeatable. For example, at the department level, shared practices for managing the IT brand might include the following:

- Reply to all urgent messages within 1-4 hours. Respond to all non-urgent messages within 24 hours. Provide a personal handoff to the right team or service center if the request or question needs to be handed off.
- Plan any out-of-office time with resource managers and team members, and communicate planned time off with customers.
- Ensure work and commitments are covered when out of the office. Set an out-of-office autoreply with contacts and escalations.
- Accept or decline all meeting requests received to help others with planning necessary collaboration.
- Keep contact information current, including mobile phone, and include this information in an email signature.
- Arrive at meetings on time and participate without distraction by turning off laptops and smartphones, or by using these tools only for meeting-related purposes (not multitasking).

• Use standard templates for all projects deliverables, presentations, meetings, and so on.

Creating a framework for each team

At the individual team level (technical service center), the goal is also to provide everyone with a common framework to follow. For example, if the value-proposition for customer support is white-glove service, the behaviors expected from all team members might include the following:

• Respond to all incident reports or requests immediately to set expectations in accordance with the agreed-upon service-level agreements (SLAs).

• For emergency issues, a customer can contact any IT team member directly, and that team member will assist in routing the customer to the correct process and/or team member to address their question.

• After closing any incident or request, the team member will follow up by email to ensure the matter has been solved and provide a contact for escalation if the customer is not satisfied.

• All problems are fixed right the first time versus quickly. The goal is no repeat incidents and preventing future problems through root cause analysis.

When organizations move to automation or outsourcing, the brand promise changes, and human interaction might be replaced with automated messages, such as "Please open an incident ticket and our team will contact you." In some cases, the client relationship suffers when customers perceive their requests for assistance falling into an abyss. Depending on the agreed-upon value proposition, organizations need to decide whether to continue to provide direct access to IT through email, IM, phone, text, or maybe even in person. At a minimum, any ticketing system must provide real time status on any incident or request. The key is to avoid any disconnect between the IT strategy (reduce costs) and the brand promise.

Even as a member of IT, I have fallen victim to the incident tracking labyrinth, feeling lost in a maze of teams, systems, and approvals to get a simple task performed or problem resolved. In some cases, users are required to use multiple systems for different teams to access IT services. IT needs to look at its services through the eyes of its clients and develop a holistic approach to manage the expectations of the user community.

For portfolio, project, and solution management, the brand may be slightly different than operations. To ensure customers and other IT shared services receive the same experience, guidelines for project and solution managers might include the following:

- Team members shall respond to all emails or requests (both customer and IT) within 24 hours, either addressing the request or acknowledging the communication and setting expectations for taking action.
- All formal meetings with internal IT, vendors, and customers will have an agenda, start on time, be facilitated effectively, end on time, and provide a recap with agreements and action items.
- All projects will provide weekly status reports, including issues, escalations, and steps taken to remedy or mitigate risks.
- All proposals and estimates for projects (business requests) will be completed within 30 days of receipt. If the scope of the business request does not allow this, a 90-day formal project blueprint will be scheduled to perform the assessment.
- IT will honor the original estimates and costs unless formal change control has occurred and been approved in writing by the stakeholder.

A good brand and reputation serves as a magnet to attract and retain a talented workforce, creating a culture where people compete to get on teams and fight to stay there. For example, the Google brand is a playful culture that uses cutting-edge innovation to attract the cream of the crop. Google receives over one million applications a year for a coveted 1,000-4,000 positions it posts. This level of attraction is an example how a brand can improve an IT organization's overall performance by defining the culture and expectations of the workforce with a simple set of ideas around the value they bring.

Building the Individual Brand of IT Employees

Each of us has a brand, although we may not know it. An individual brand is the association people make with his or her name.

Because the IT brand is the aggregate of all its customer-facing team members, successful IT organizations encourage those behaviors that promote one's individual brand and thereby the IT brand as a whole improves.

For example, an outage or incident isn't always what devalues the IT brand. During times of critical need and times when everything is operating smoothly, how IT is managed, day-to-day, is what is critical to maintaining the IT brand. Every phone call made, every meeting attended, every email sent by the IT workforce influences how peers and customers experience IT. The IT brand can be tarnished when resources do not follow through on commitments, write ineffective emails, do not take appropriate responsibility for mistakes, or just forget to set an out-of-office reminder and something goes wrong while they're away.

Keep in mind, it is not just the call center that determines the customer experience. The reality is that IT resources talk to each other and with customers on a daily basis, sharing messages about their organization to the world around them. Work ethic, actions, and the individual beliefs of all IT resources shape the perception of IT services both internally and externally. Further, when IT resources are frustrated, they might communicate this across their peer group and sometimes to clients directly or indirectly in their engagement style. Disengaged resources do not provide the same value and loyalty as engaged employees. Managers need to ensure everyone is following the same scripts when performing their duties or else counterproductive messaging will create drag on the organization.

Most friction and resistance can be removed with effective marketing of the IT brand to build trust. However, organizations must also teach employees how to manage their individual brands. Posters, slogans, icons, and logos are the easy part of branding. The hard part is changing behaviors. Therefore organizations can improve their brand by providing the roadmap for resources to do the inner/outer work needed make any personal transformation required to align behaviors with the IT brand. These behaviors include how one listens, communicates, and develops his or her image. Think of managing the individual brand as a personal assessment for skills, competencies, and values.

Taking the first steps

Although many factors go into developing one's personal brand, here are four that can improve one's brand immediately:

1. Understand how to work a room

How is that some people just seem to float through a room at professional events, working their way from each small group, never staying too long in one place and always having something interesting to discuss, a question to ask, or a witty comment. These individuals always appear graceful, poised, and articulate.

In 2012, before a big offsite management event, I decided to do some homework and came across this bestselling book on how to work a room. (See *How to Work a Room* by Susan RoAne in the upcoming resources section.) RoAne's book explained the benefits of socializing as well as the problems typically encountered when doing so. This included exploring common problems we all face and practical advice using specific examples.

After taking time to get some tips about how to circulate the room, entering and exiting conversations gracefully, I found these events more enjoyable and beneficial to my brand. Figuring out the social science of working a room not only helped me polish these skills for events, but also feel more comfortable in all social situations, including working with internal and external clients.

2. Polish your email communication skills.

Most of us probably spend more time reading and writing emails in a given week than all other tasks combined. So it's surprising how little investment we make to polish this competency. Email is probably the largest contributor to one's personal brand, and it is the single fastest way to improve your brand through effective editing.

For me, I realized I needed to treat email like writing an essay: Get the ideas down, and then edit, edit, and edit again. Remove unnecessary language, be precise, get to the point, be specific, and commit to the position. The goal is to write emails to help your audience understand your message or question and receive accurate and timely answers to inquiries.

For help with email communication skills, I recommend *Email at the Workplace* by Juan Carlos Jiménez, discussed in the upcoming resources section.

3. Run effective meetings.

Running effective meetings is critical to developing and managing your individual brand. We have all heard people complain of too many meetings or poorly run meetings. However, like email, meetings are a big part of work life. If you can learn to run meetings that are exciting, deal with real issues, and promote healthy debate, you can help your colleagues find the best solutions in the shortest amount of time.

More importantly, if you cannot manage meetings that facilitate these type of discussions, people will notice. In contrast, when you are able to bring enthusiasm and stimulate your colleagues to collaborate quickly to solve technical or business problems, people will also notice — in a positive way! Running a productive meeting that keeps people engaged is an art form.

To improve your skills in running and participating in meetings, I recommend *Death by Meeting* by Patrick M. Lencioni.

4. Commit to your craft first and then to your career ambitions

You can manage your career or manage your craft. Whichever you choose, others will notice, and your choice will become part of your brand. I advocate managing one's craft first because high-performing employees are an essential building block of great organizations. They are the ones who figure out what to do when there is no rule book or instructions to follow. They are humble, not self-promoting or worried about recognition, and that is why they're indispensable.

One does not have to be the smartest person in the room to be a high performer. You just need to be someone who genuinely loves the challenge of your work, is committed, and turns what you do each day into a kind of art. Because high-performers don't seek recognition, they are highly respected in their organizations. I believe by taking what you do every day to an art form, you open more doors than if you worry about career advancement.

When you apply all your cognitive thinking power to the job you have versus the one you want, the universe has a strange way opening those doors desired or perhaps ones you never knew existed.

Remember that successful consulting firms groom consultants with competencies that build trust and client loyalty. These firms coach consultants for interviews and seek regular feedback from clients on their performance. In the competitive IT industry, consultants must be articulate and highly productive while embracing uncommon levels of humility, selflessness, and transparency for the good of the client. The great thing is, the first step in managing your personal brand is self-awareness and simply starting to observe the brand of others.

Finding resources for developing an individual brand

Although developing an individual brand is a book unto itself, this section catalogues some influential authors who can provide insights on how to improve one's interpersonal and leadership skills as well as other resources.

What Got You Here Won't Get You There
by Marshall Goldsmith

In *What Got You Here Won't Get You There,* Goldsmith explains 20 common flaws of interpersonal behavior that can lead to flaws in leadership behaviors. The author suggests that correcting these behaviors does not require polished skills, training, arduous practice, or supernatural creativity. Rather, if you recognize any of these behaviors in yourself, you just need an awareness of how this behavior holds you back in order to stop doing what you have done in the past. Here a few examples of the workplace habits to avoid:

- **Adding too much value:** This is the overwhelming desire to add one's two cents to every discussion.

- **Telling the world how smart one is:** Sometimes, when individuals don't feel valued, they attempt to show people they're smarter than others think.

- **Negativity, or "Let me explain why that won't work":** Some folks need to share their negative thoughts even when they weren't asked.

- **Withholding information:** Here, Goldsmith is talking specifically about refusing to share information in order to maintain an advantage over others.

- **Failing to give proper recognition:** Some people are either too caught up in the next task or deadline or simply don't think to offer praise and reward, even though praise is among the simplest and most inexpensive incentives a manager can offer.

- **Clinging to the past:** In this self-preservation tactic, people deflect blame away from themselves and onto events and people from their past. This behavior a subset of blaming everyone else.

Self-assessing the 20 common flaws is a great starting point for doing the inner work necessary to identify — and ultimately promote — your personal brand. The first step is recognizing and acknowledging one is capable of this behavior instead of denying, justifying, and disowning it. Some people might benefit from a trusted advisor, mentor, or friend who can be honest about their blind spots — the things others can see but that are hard to see in oneself. As painful as this inner work can be, missing your blind spots can easily tarnish your brand and reduce your effectiveness.

How to Work a Room *by Susan RoAne*

RoAne breaks down these problems one by one and offers practical advice using specific examples. As I mentioned earlier, when I was on my way to a manager offsite event, I decided to read this book on the airplane. I made notes to myself and even picked up a newspaper and magazine to get familiar with current events in case the conversation turned to something other than work.

The trick I learned was to realize before even entering the room, I already had many things in common with other people — even strangers or casual acquaintances. We all had to travel somehow to get to the conference. We were all staying at the same hotel, having drinks, eating the same food, and attending for the same reason. I found I could quickly identify five or six questions that were very relevant for anyone new I met. Furthermore, with some effective listening skills, I could probably come up with several follow-up questions, such as, "You do not care for this hotel?," "Where do like to stay when you travel?," or "What airlines do you usually use?"

Historically at these events, I would find some people I know, near the bar of course, and have a one-to-three hour social while enjoying as many spirits as was reasonable and socially acceptable. However, RoAne gave tips and suggestions about how to circulate the room, entering and exiting conversations gracefully. I found this book effortless to read, funny, and very relevant. Another pearl of wisdom was how to develop a ten-second speech about who I am, including how to have fun and make it memorable. Because this speech is the first thing you say, it should be brief and well-rehearsed.

Learning the etiquette of active listening, asking qualifying questions, and graceful interaction with others improves the personal and IT brand alike.

Email at the Workplace by Juan Carlos Jiménez

As noted earlier, email is the number one method of workplace communication but rarely looked as a competency that one needs to grow and improve. However, email is the low-hanging fruit that can have a large impact on how peers and customers perceive you. In this book, Jiménez explains ways to make your emails more effective. Here are just a few ways he helps readers evaluate and improve their email communications:

- Is the subject line specific to help people easily manage this message in their email inbox as well as prioritize their response?
- Is the key point and the action required stated in the beginning?
- Do you use white space to separate ideas and paragraphs?
- What is the writing style? Aim for 1 idea per paragraph and 15-20 words per sentence. Also, emphasize the point early or at the end.
- Is the most important thought in the first paragraph?
- Who is on the To: line or CC: line and why are they included?
- Before responding to an email, have you edited your response to remove all emotional material that could be misunderstood?

These are just a few examples of email best practices that can help people communicate effectively. Many books out there can help you learn or improve the way you structure emails and understand writing and communication principles. When your emails follow these best practices, you can help your audience understand your message or question and receive more timely answers to inquiries.

The goal of building out this writing competency is to look at the email paradigm from both perspectives — the sender and the receiver. Some of these tips are simple, such as the following:

- If you have trouble proofreading your own emails, don't send them right away. Walk away and come back. If you are upset, send the message to yourself or a friend to proof before distributing it more widely.
- If you sometimes send rapid-fire emails back to back, perhaps your thoughts are not complete or the messages are not clearly articulated.
- If no one responds to your email, find out why by picking up the phone. Maybe the email was not clear about who was responsible; for example, have you ever seen an email with six people on the To: line and a statement or action not addressed to a single team member?

Fine-tuning email communication can be one of the most valuable investments an individual can make to polish his or her brand.

Death by Meeting *by Patrick M. Lencioni*

Death by Meeting chronicles the art of meeting facilitation. Running effective meetings is critical to developing and managing your individual brand. After reading this book, I became acutely aware of how so many meetings I attend lacked focus, do not discuss topics that are important, or venture down rabbit holes on irrelevant topics. Also, I started looking around to see who is participating and who is not. As it turns out, I was not alone. I need only observe people's body language and facial expressions or look for people working away on other tasks and/or on their iPhone.

Running a productive meeting that keeps people engaged is an art form. Therefore, this book is recommended for anyone who attends or manages meetings on a regular basis.

Keep in mind, you don't have to be the facilitator to drive efficiencies in how your time is used. After reading this book, I developed this list of ground rules for meetings I conduct or attend:

- **Set the meeting context in an agenda and invite:** Often I get meeting invites with no agenda or objectives spelled out. If unclear, begin with asking "Why you are having this meeting?" Is it strategic, staff, checkpoint, problem solving, or some other reason?
- **Come prepared:** If it's your meeting, let people know how to prepare. Explain the purpose and ask them to do research and preparation ahead of time. A little preliminary work greatly improves the quality of any

discussion and the decisions that result from the initial meeting.

- **Don't fear conflict:** Conflict at times can be uncomfortable. However, healthy conflict is necessary and is nothing more than a business problem that needs to be resolved. Maybe acknowledge each point of view but do not insist everyone agree.

- **Don't strive for consensus:** The likelihood of a group of people coming to a complete agreement on a complex and important strategic topic is very low. If fact if everyone always agrees on everything, this might be symptomatic of a different problem in the culture.

- **Value debate:** Advocate unfiltered, provocative, passionate discussions that end when a leader decides all the information has been aired. Set this expectation up front. Clarify that everyone has an opportunity to share their views but that a specific individual or group will make the final decision.

- **Gain commitment:** Regardless of what position people originally took, after the decision is made, ensure everyone supports the decision. Remember, this is a business transaction, and there are no winners and losers.

- **Show respect:** Manage all confrontation productively and effectively while maintaining positive working relationships. Leaders must model the right behavior and hold employees and peers accountable for unprofessional behavior.

In addition to *Death by Meeting,* Patrick M. Lencioni has written a number of books, all catering to idea of improving an organization's health. But these books can also can improve one's personal brand. Here is a short list of books that can be helpful in shaping one's values and approach to engaging peers, clients, and executive leadership:

- *Getting Naked* teaches the consulting mindset through a lens of humility and providing value.

- *Silos, Politics and Turf War* is a great book for middle managers who want to understand the dynamics that reduce productivity across verticals in the organization.

- *The Five Dysfunctions of a Team* is a clever leadership story that illustrates how to drive more trust and accountability within a team.

Linchpin *by Seth Godin*

The premise of this book is that linchpins are the essential building blocks of great organizations. Like the small piece of hardware that keeps a wheel from falling off its axle, they may not be famous, but they're indispensable. And in today's world, they gain the best jobs and the most freedom.

The goal of the book is to show you how to become a linchpin in your organization. Linchpins don't have to be geniuses, but rather someone who loves the challenge of their work, is committed, and turns what they do each day into a kind of art. What's important to me about this book is how it turns the focus inward, to your own personal development and job satisfaction. Also, this book recognizes that the potential for greatness is in each of us!

Toastmasters presentations (or other similar programs)

Communication and presentations are a big part of IT work. The number-one fear employees have is public speaking, and an important skill recruiters look for is the ability to communicate effectively. Clients want to work with IT resources who express themselves clearly and confidently. To successfully manage the IT brand in an organization, IT resources must be both persuasive and comfortable communicating with a wide range of people, from top executives to system users. This means their confidence and personal intensity enables them to influence others. Although many books and courses cover this topic, in this section, I talk about Toastmasters, which offers a Competent Communicator Certification to help individuals groom this skill set.

Toastmasters is not a class, trade school, or university. Rather, it's a learning environment where members both advanced and novice come together to polish their skills by following a proven discipline. The meeting format is a combination of participating in two-minute Table Topics and preparing and giving six- to eight-minute speeches in front of the group. All speeches are scheduled in advance and feedback is provided during the meeting on what went well and areas for improvement. After you successfully complete 10 speeches, you receive a certification as a Competent Communicator. The speeches get harder and build on the skills acquired in the previous speech. The first speech is a simple ice breaker and the last is "inspiring your audience." This is a great place work out distracting behaviors, like swaying, putting your hands in your pockets, leaning on the podium, speaking in a monotone, lacking a sense of humor, or being overly emotional or intense during a presentation.

Public speaking is part of managing your personal brand. The best way to improve your skills is by practicing giving presentations. If you get butterflies before public speaking, consider joining Toastmasters or a similar program that can help with speech anxiety, stage fright, and platform panic. As a starting point, Toastmasters has these suggestions:

- **Know the room:** Arrive early, become familiar with the room, and test equipment, such as the microphone. If time permits, put up your presentation and walk around the room to ensure everyone can see it.

- **Know the audience:** If possible, greet members as they arrive, ask their names, and chat with them. It's easier to speak to a group of friends than strangers.

- **Know your material:** If you are not familiar with your material, your nervousness will increase. You can be easily thrown off your game.

- **Practice a few relaxation techniques:** There are a number of techniques to ground yourself before a presentation, including deep breathing, stretching, facial exercises, vocal exercises, and whatever helps you relax.

- **Visualize yourself giving the speech:** Athletes do this in preparation for an event. Visualize yourself walking to the lectern and facing the audience. Imagine yourself speaking, using hand gestures, and gliding across the stage. Visualize success.

- **Realize that people want you to succeed:** Audiences want speakers to be interesting, stimulating, informative, and entertaining.

- **Don't apologize if you make a mistake:** Most of the time, your nervousness does not even show up to the audience. If you don't admit a mistake, they won't know it happened. If you lose your place, don't freak out; just gaze up thoughtfully, even if it takes many seconds. The time doesn't seem as long for your audience as it feels to you. Apologizing may just call attention to something nobody noticed.

- **Concentrate on the message — not on the medium:** Remind yourself what you are here to do. You have scrubbed the presentation multiple times and rehearsed your content and delivery. Channel any remaining fear and anxiety into communicating the message.

Chapter Summary

An IT brand clarifies the IT value proposition throughout the business. The brand is an important tool in managing relationships with both internal and external IT customers. The IT brand also ensures that effective communication supports the IT strategy, thereby seeding a culture where IT teams and projects are more likely to not only be successful, but also be *perceived* as successful.

IT leaders need to communicate to the IT workforce the importance of managing the IT brand. Creating awareness of expectations ensures repeatable and consistent behaviors when dealing with IT clients.

Giving individuals the opportunity to understand and develop their personal brand can help employees support the IT brand in their day-to-day interactions with IT customers. When developing an individual brand, consider the characteristics you admire the most in other IT professionals and then develop a strategy to polish those skill sets. Further, when you're not exactly sure where to look, it's helpful to read books that have resonated with other IT workers across the industry or seek help from a career coach or mentor.

Remember, the idea of a brand is to create an association of trust and value with the consumer of your products and services. Customers should associate the brand (and each individual that represents the brand) with an experience they expect on every engagement. IT leadership can help set this expectation by giving the IT workforce a framework and communication guidelines that support the brand and by delivering on all commitments.

Managing the IT brand is about aligning the actual outcomes with the IT promise.

PART IV

SIXTH PROTOCOL:
ORGANIZATIONAL HEALTH

CHAPTER 10

ENGAGING EMPLOYEES

Some fear among employees is good: fear of a deadline, fear of providing needed functionality, even fear of reputation can motivate employees to put their best foot forward. However, the type of fear and uncertainty that profit-based strategies seed can paralyze employees, reduce productivity, and impact IT's value proposition, because how IT employees experience their jobs determines how they interact with the clients of IT.

This chapter shines on light on the ways profit-based strategies can lead to management practices and a workplace culture that alienate employees. To remove these problems, IT leadership needs to understand what truly motivates employees and then use that understanding to facilitate management and employee-development practices that create an engaged workforce.

Undermining Engagement with Profit-Based Management Strategies and Poor Workplace Culture

Today, more than ever, job satisfaction is at all-time lows, and often this dissatisfaction is a result of both management style and culture. Profit-based strategies put undue pressure on managers to drive cost savings, thereby impacting employees and distracting them from focusing on what's important (serving the clients of IT). In turn, employees' inability to get actual work done undermines their trust in management, and threats of layoffs from outsourcing and downsizing exacerbates the problem.

Identifying management practices that alienate employees

According to a press release, social media–based recruitment agency staff-bay.com surveyed 15,000 jobseekers and found that 87.2 percent of respondents said they wanted to leave their current job sometime in 2014. When asked why, more than half — 52.6 percent — said it was because they did not trust their boss. Tony Wilmot, cofounder of staffbay.com, said, "What the survey shows us is that there is a breakdown between employee and employer. Many of the respondents to our survey said they simply don't trust their boss to do the right thing by them and their career. Others felt they weren't valued at all."

A 2013 Gallup poll found that 7 out of 10 Americans hate their jobs. More than half of workers — 52 percent — are not engaged in their work, with another 18 percent reporting that they are actively disengaged from their jobs. According to Gallup, this disengagement costs U.S. companies up to $550 billion per year in lost productivity. Gallup also found that workplace disengagement is largely a result of bosses either completely ignoring workers or focusing too much on employees' weaknesses.

A new poll conducted by Maritz Research discovered a lack of trust in not only senior leaders, but also in direct managers and coworkers. According to the poll:

- Only 11 percent of employees believe their managers show consistency between their words and their actions.
- Only 7 percent of employees trust senior leaders to look out for their best interests.
- 80 percent of respondents do not believe their company leaders are completely honest and ethical.
- Only 25 percent of respondents trust management to make the right decisions in times of uncertainty.

From these polls, employees' trust in management is clearly deteriorating because employees don't feel valued, receive more criticism than positive support and development, and question their employers' ethics and decision-making processes.

Some of these workplace trends around employee dissatisfaction are a symptom of the shift in company priorities from finding and retaining top talent to finding and retaining candidates who will champion profit-driven behaviors. For example, earlier in this book, I discuss the following problems with profit-based strategies:

- Profit-based performance metrics often focus on number of tickets closed but do not give IT employees time to perform root cause analysis to fix the underlying issues. As a result, employees don't trust the metrics that IT and business leadership are promoting, because employees are keenly aware that they're wasting time and energy fixing the same issue over and over instead of finding a lasting solution to a problem.

- Profit-based outsourcing strategies may reduce costs on paper only. Although these solutions have a significant impact on the careers of everyone in the organization, the experience is often a positive one only for leadership and vendors implementing these changes. The employees left managing the outsourcing engagements have a negative experience.

- When companies do not invest in staffing or technology to sustain the growth of customers and users, "the cheap always comes out expensive" in rework, remediation, reputation, and employee dissatisfaction.

Sometimes, these downsides of profit-based strategies cost the organization its most valuable asset: high-performing employees.

Without credible leadership, employees don't buy in to the corporate mission and vision, resulting in a disengaged workforce that puts self-interest first.

Understanding the dark side of workplace culture

In April 2015, Brad Reed wrote an article for BGR titled "Apple employee quits his job, spills dirt on 'what really goes on' there." This story chronicles how an ex-Apple employee named Ben Farrell quit his job at Apple and wrote a scathing blog post about what it's really like to work for the company.

Farrell's list of reasons for quitting provides a comprehensive list of workplace-culture issues that alienate employees: excessively long hours, unproductive meetings, lack of sympathy for family emergencies, in-fighting, backstabbing, and more. However, this is not to say all of Apple's culture is this way.

All of us have experienced or at least known of someone who has worked in a department or a company that expects employees to work excessively long days and/or weekends. But dark cultures are more than just long hours. In these environments:

- Employees expend great amounts of energy to trip up their peers rather than collaborate on finding solutions.

- Both sender and receiver scrutinize every word in every email for a possible double meaning.
- Every presentation is sanitized to protect the innocent
- No meaningful information is ever shared that improves the client's condition.

When leadership allows a toxic culture like this to thrive, employees find themselves attending meetings to prepare for meetings sometimes in preparation for other meetings. Employees and leaders alike can end up spending an excessive amount of time doing damage control, creating reports, and sifting through emails to find evidence for a counter attack. All the while, their peers, colleagues, and customers stand by helplessly watching, waiting and questioning who is the adult at this table.

Douglas LaBier, author of *Modern Madness: The Hidden Link between Work and Emotional Conflict,* calls employees like Farrell "the working wounded, healthy people adjusted at great emotional cost due to conditions that are good for the advancement of the career but not the spirit." (However, as many employees eventually do, Farrell ultimately quit instead of adjusting to the workplace culture.)

LaBier points out that working success often just represents adaptation and fitting into the collective persona of an organization by burying those qualities that don't fit into the real company culture. Further, when companies reward the wrong behaviors and have a low tolerance for critical feedback from employees, employees are faced with a painful conflicts of values when expected to violate their principles, dominate others, tell white lies, or sell out in other small ways. The pressure of these cultures can lead employees to make bargains at great costs to themselves, because the culture makes employees feel uncomfortable challenging their peers or management.

What Really Motivates Employees?

The first step in addressing the problem of employee engagement is to understand what truly motivates people, including their beliefs systems and values. Like company leadership, employees also are faced with tough decisions every day that have consequences. When work values do not align with personal ethics, work can become a repetitive chore and thankless exertion in order to provide a livelihood. This holds true for IT factory workers providing low-cost IT services as well as the corporate executives who find their roles dutiful and meaningless.

Many of us long to renew a sense of purpose in our work while feeling safe to be creative, take risks, and make mistakes. But this sense of purpose and safety is not possible when employees are asked to sacrifice passion for security and at times, even participate in scapegoating others who do not conform to the rules in order to fit into the collective mold.

To survive, employees ultimately must create a persona for work by surrendering their individuality in order to wear the white hat (one who is admired and respected by management). The employees who are unable to create this imaginary persona eventually become frustrated and disengaged, often leaving the company in search of work with a more value-based culture.

What companies fail to understand is that losing talented employees can be very expensive. Laszlo Bock, Google's Senior Vice-President of People Operations and author of *Work Rules! Insights from Google That Will Transform How You Live and Lead*, noted that most companies don't know how to hold onto their best people and that "People don't stay for the money." Bock goes on to explain that the following aspects of workplace culture are what motivate employees:

- **The quality of the people they work with:** Bock emphasizes the importance of hiring. Google sets a high standard for everyone it hires. Whether you're applying for an administrative assistant position or that of senior engineer, every candidate is screened by their potential boss, potential colleagues, a hiring committee, and finally Google CEO Larry Page.
- **The feeling that the work they do is meaningful:** Bock works from the belief that people look for meaning in their work. Plus, giving employees a sense of purpose has benefits beyond retention. Bock cites research by Wharton professor Adam Grant that found when people are able to connect their jobs to something meaningful, their productivity increases as much as five times.

In addition to Bock's insights, I explain earlier in this book that how employees are measured, compensated, and rewarded can drive the behaviors and effect outcomes (good and bad). Perhaps the third ingredient to add to Bock's list on how to motivate employees is the right performance-management and compensation program. In other words, employees don't work *only* for the money.

In addition to a quality team and meaningful work, employees need to trust the performance-management approach. When employees do not trust the measurements or compensation is unequal, commitment and productivity suffer. However, the money isn't necessarily about how much compensation each employee receives, but rather how the company manages the rewards and compensation program itself that determines whether the employee feels his or her relative contribution is valued. I explore rewards and compensation in more detail in Chapter 11.

Creating a Culture That Improves Employee Engagement

If companies are to reverse the trends in the workplace that can result in dehumanizing the culture, employers must change the dynamic and foster the authenticity needed while removing the fear of losing one's job.

How management can help

Developing a sound IT roadmap and strategy is not enough. Organizations require an equal emphasis on employee engagement, culture, and personal development to ensure employees see the connection between work and the value it brings. Companies need to find new and creative ways to help employees stay engaged, get behind the company's business and IT strategy, and build a sense of trust in the organization. This is accomplished through active employee engagement and when leadership models the behaviors for employees to emulate.

Active employee engagement means developing a hands-on approach to managing how employees experience their jobs. Ethics training and posters about culture do not translate into trust or an engaged workforce. Companies must walk the walk.

However, providing additional leadership training, SOPs about organizational culture, and announcing generally at all hands meetings how employees are valued are topical treatments that do not give people a sense of purpose or belonging. In contrast, the following methods provide employees a direct experience that can translate into trust and commitment of the workforce:

- **Creating a regular opportunity for one-on-one feedback:** The most important tool managers have to engage employees is their time. Managers can set up regular one-on-one meetings to discuss what the employee is working on and the challenges they face, provide advice, and review goals the employee has for personal development. These meetings should not be a status meeting for the benefit of the manager. Rather, the time should be focused on developing a more personal connection with the associate and letting them provide the manager with insights on how they are feeling about their job, accomplishments, or areas for improvement. Throughout these one-on-one meetings, the manager needs to practice active listening.

- **Talking openly about negative emotions:** Employees should be encouraged to express concerns openly and honestly. Managers can have empathy without taking responsibility for employee feelings. Further, managers can be transparent about what organizational problems they can and will address, and those that are not within the manager's control due to constraints. The reality is, every employee and manager alike will someday be faced with a painful conflicts of values or choices. The responsibility of a manager is to guide employees through the difficult times with grace and self-respect.

- **Addressing the real problems employees are struggling with:** As noted earlier in the book, strategy and culture both contribute significantly to the quality of life for the employee. Aging systems that fail often, understaffing of teams to save money, and excessive politics due to a poorly designed IT ecosystem all contribute to reduced employee satisfaction and productivity. Architecting an IT strategy that identifies and addresses real problems that employees face on the front line will increase commitment and employee engagement. Conversely, a profit-based strategy that does not take into consideration the real problems faced by employees will increase conflict, tarnish the IT brand, and create additional drag on an IT organization already struggling to deliver on its commitments.

Helping individuals grow

To recover the buried potential of the organization, IT leadership should consider creating a program that fosters more direct contact with their employee population. Here are some examples of how management can promote each employee's development:

- As noted in Chapter 9, in the section on managing one's personal brand, organizations need to develop programs to teach employees those critical survival skills not part of college or technical school curriculum.

- Management should find more opportunities for associates to get face time with senior leaders to develop and present recommendations on IT projects and initiatives. Managers and senior leadership can use these meetings as mentoring opportunities and a chance to let employee grow and showcase their knowledge and skills.

- Include associates in the ITBM planning, IT roadmap development, staffing assessments, budget planning, and other IT planning activities. This involvement gives employees more transparency into how decisions are being made and prepares them for their next move upward into the organization.

The common thread here is that leadership needs to spend more time making a personal connection with the workforce. This includes observing and helping individuals understand how their personal behavior contributes both positively and negatively to the environment around them. By encouraging employees to self-reflect on their behaviors in the workplace, new levels of growth are possible including the following:

- Achieving a genuine self-acceptance based on a complete knowledge of who they are and their strengths and weaknesses
- Defusing negative emotions that erupt unexpectedly in their daily lives and giving them tools to navigate these turbulent waters
- Healing relationships through honest self-examination and direct communications, such as having the humility to admit mistakes
- Recognizing how their projections (that is, their own feelings) color their opinions of others

A Case Study in Employee Engagement: SmallBox

SmallBox is a company that has found ways to effectively balance company growth with employee engagement. "The culture for SmallBox evolved out of necessity due to rapid growth," explains Sara McGuyer, Chief Culture Officer. This employee engagement program resulted in a thematic goal of deepening existing client relationships rather than focusing on growth for profit. "As a result, this was a game-changer which had unexpected benefits when it magnetized new clients towards us."

Over the past five years, SmallBox has launched a number of initiatives, such as the 24-Hour Web Project (nicknamed 24HWP) and Factory Week. 24HWP was intended to create a culture of giving, but also had the unexpected result of positively impacting their business growth. Factory Week was designed to give employees time to work together closely on a big-picture problem. Both of these initiatives have created a sense of belonging and common purpose for employees.

24-Hour Web Project

24HWP is an annual event where SmallBox teams come together to pull an all-nighter and build a website for a local nonprofit as a donation. The intention of the program is to drive increased trust and collaboration across teams by giving them a common goal as well as a deadline. Although 24HWP was not intended as a marketing strategy, it ended up driving new business to the company because a large portion of the company's portfolio are nonprofit organizations.

SmallBox just completed year five of this program. Employees look forward to it like a vacation: It's a time for them to come together around a larger purpose and put their talents into action in a very real and meaningful way. McGuyer points out that these types of events really showcase the Small-Box culture. The company recognizes that an all-nighter isn't something that could be pulled off very often if the company is to maintain balance for employees' personal lives. But from the employees' perspective, all agree that the annual all-nighter is worthwhile, because at the end of the day, an amazing nonprofit receives a powerful new tool to do good work in the world, and the SmallBox team has stretched and grown, finding new ways to collaborate and deliver.

Factory Week

In another example of getting employees aligned behind common goals, Factory Week was born out of the desire to focus on ideas and projects that make SmallBox a better company. SmallBox modeled Factory Week after Andy Warhol's studio, the Factory, famous for groundbreaking gatherings between artists and musicians. The SmallBox team loved the dynamic that image produced — coming together and collaborating in ways that produced great things. The idea with Factory Week is that all client work (except support) is put on hold, so that teams can focus on priorities that employees normally don't have time to drive forward. McGuyer used the anecdote, "The company did not want to be the cobbler with really bad shoes."

These are just two examples of how companies balance company's goals and objectives with employee engagement. In both examples, the company and employees end up with a win-win experience.

Chapter Summary

To resolve problems with employee disengagement, companies need to understand and change the management practices that alienate employees most as well as the company cultures that reward these bad management practices. When developing a strategy for employee engagement, senior leadership and managers need to consider the following:

- Surveys have shown that employees' trust in management is deteriorating because employees don't feel valued, receive more criticism than positive support or individual development, and question their employers' ethics and decision-making processes.
- When companies reward the wrong behaviors and have a low tolerance for critical feedback from employees, employees are faced with a painful

conflicts of values that can reduce productivity and cost the company its high-performing employees.

- Managers need to grow organizational talent by observing and helping individuals understand how their personal behavior contributes both positively and negatively to the environment.

- Active employee engagement means developing a hands-on approach to managing how employees experience their jobs. This includes
  - Creating ongoing opportunities for one-on-one feedback
  - Talking openly about negative emotions
  - Addressing the real problems with which employees struggle

CHAPTER 11

REWARDS AND COMPENSATION

In IT organizations, attracting and retaining high-potential and top-performing employees can be the single most important investment the company will ever make. However, traditional performance-management programs often undermine this investment by promoting competition for higher salaries and bonuses among employees. Unintentionally, these competition-based programs can hurt the team dynamic, inhibit creativity, reduce overall productivity, and create distrust or frustration with the performance-based metrics, which in turn hurts employee engagement.

To counteract these problems and protect the company's investment in its employees, IT leadership can add value-based management practices to the company's performance-management program. These practices include connecting with employees, offering career-growth opportunities, and creating transparency and honesty around performance-management metrics.

These value-based practices can help the company stand out from the crowd: Most high-performing employees value the work they do over the level compensation received because, for similar skills sets at the individual contributor and lower management levels, the variance in pay tends to be small between companies. Further, for these employees, the decision to join or stay at a company is not tied exclusively to the compensation they receive, but fueled as much by nonmonetary rewards.

For example, I recently did a tour consulting with eBay and PayPal. The office spaces sported ping-pong tables, foosball tables, and common collaboration areas with couches and white boards. Instead of assigning offices to managers, all rooms were conference rooms. In fact everything about the organization encouraged employees to work and even play together. The PayPal campus included multiple cafeterias, volleyball courts (with sand), basketball courts, a soccer field, and wireless access from anywhere in the campus, enabling workers to sit outside and conduct their meetings if desired. You were never sure who the senior leaders or C-Level executives were because everyone had a tendency to wear jeans to work. The culture attracted employees to this company. Employees genuinely enjoyed their work and were proud of the company, which made them a magnet for attracting and retaining top talent.

Exploring the Pitfalls of Traditional Performance-Management Programs

Today, in companies around the world, most employers have established a framework that rewards the highest performers with the highest share of rewards. Incentives like bonuses, merit increases, and stock options are woven into the fabric of the compensation strategy to motivate employees to compete against each other. The belief system is that all employees desire more money and recognition so they will work harder than their colleagues to achieve those goals, thereby driving up overall productivity in exchange for rewards. The strategy is simple: just a carrot, a stick, and a piece of string to dangle the reward is all that is needed to create a high-performance framework.

Business leaders who believe internal competition drives higher productivity may be surprised with the industry data collected on this topic over the last few decades. For example, salespeople taken off a commission-based compensation model actually collaborate more, share leads, and increase revenue significantly higher than in a commission-based model. By placing all salespeople on salary, this removes the pressure of having to make the sale, enabling the salesperson to have a more genuine, warm, and inviting style when engaging the client.

Inhibiting teamwork and creativity

The problem with giving the highest share of rewards to the few is the conditioning of employees that productivity, creativity, and an innovative mindset is tied to the reward itself. This encourages employees to compete with each other instead of collaborating with each other, because in order to receive rewards, one must exceed the ability of one's peers. This competition has far-reaching psychological implications when a company is trying to create a team dynamic.

Further, the fear itself of not receiving a reward inhibits some associates from asking for help, letting managers know when they are in over their heads, or making them risk averse. Employees are caught in a dichotomy when managers ask employees to raise the bar, innovate, and think outside of the box but then grade them down when, in the process of doing so, they ask for help, make a mistake, or have to perform rework on an assignment or project. Fear of reputation among peers and the fear of being criticized by one's manager can cripple team members' creativity and productivity on the job.

Daniel H. Pink describes this phenomenon in his book *Drive: The Truth about What Motivates Us*, citing studies over the last 50 years on the psychological impacts of reward systems. Through his analysis of this research, Pink explores the cognitive dissonance between what science knows and what business do today — and how business practices affect employee motivation. He builds a case that, although carrots and sticks worked successfully in the twentieth century, that's precisely the wrong way to motivate people for today's challenges. Pink introduces a new belief system around performance management: The reward itself may create fear and uncertainty of not receiving the reward, thereby impacting the employee's behavior. The greater the reward an employee might lose, the more the reward inhibits and distracts the employee and thus ultimately reduces creativity and productivity.

Limiting program effectiveness with a bell curve

One last consideration is that the rewards themselves can create a dynamic that reduces productivity when employees do not trust the measurements for determining who is deserving. Performance-management programs aren't like the Olympics, where you can time the 50-yard dash or measure the distance of the javelin throw. These programs aren't even like an ice skating competition, where a panel of independent judges observe the skater directly and measure the performance against a prescribed set of common criteria.

Every year, in companies across North America and perhaps around the globe, employees enter into an implied contract with employers around performance management and rewards. Employees are told that if they push themselves, work harder than their peers, raise the bar on their contributions, and help the company hit or exceed targets, they will be rewarded handsomely.

However, the performance management framework that determines high, average, and low ratings is subjective and can be inconsistently applied across the organization. Therefore, those who believe they exceeded expectations, whether or not that belief is accurate, may fail to receive an expected reward and become disengaged and less productive.

Rarely does company leader or middle manager clarify that only a limited number of high performers are eligible based on a bell curve or quota, so only the best of the best are chosen for this honor. Although rating systems can vary from company to company, the bell curve typically falls into four categories, closely tied to compensation and rewards, as shown in Figure 11-1.

PERFORMANCE MANAGEMENT BELL CURVE

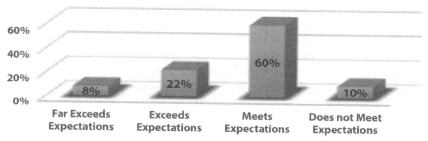

Figure 11-1

In this bell curve approach, organizations have, from the start, set the expectation that 10 percent of the population will fail. This expectation is like the Gartner fail-forward-fast strategy, which accepts project failure rates of 20-28 percent as a norm. Doing the math, in a company with 35,000 employees, roughly 3,500 employees will be low performers, unproductive, and not receive their expected compensation (merit, bonus, or stock if eligible). The company may place the employee on a Performance Improvement Plan (PIP), or manage them out of the company, incurring additional costs. This practice is not only an acceptable way to manage the people; it's part of the financial plan.

In the same example company, the bell curve predetermines that 60 percent (or 21,000 employees) are average. So up-front, the company's performance-management program creates two problems:

- **Setting low expectations:** Nearly 70 percent of the workforce will not be high performers (where 10 percent don't meet expectations and 60 percent are average).

- **Withholding rewards from deserving employees:** Because the bell curve restricts the number of high-performing employees, employees can work hard all year, thereby deserving the Exceeds Expectations rating, but due to quotas, are not awarded the coveted rating. This restriction is particularly frustrating for managers who succeed in attracting, hiring, and retaining top talent on their teams. No matter how successful the associates are, a bell curve guarantees winners and losers, often without a clear explanation of what the losing employee needed to do differently next year. Employees soon learn that in order to receive the coveted Exceeds Expectations rating, they must align themselves with teams that have less competent peers versus surrounding oneself with more talented individuals. In the end, this approach reduces trust and personal growth. Further, it creates a moral dilemma for managers who want to push direct reports towards achieving high performance goals when rewarding those reports fairly isn't possible. At times, managers are forced to mark down employees despite their relative contributions.

As noted earlier, performance-management plans are not like sports, where you know who crosses the finish line first, second, and third, and companies can prove it with a photo finish. In contrast, multiple levels of management are involved in rating and ranking employees, and sometimes, managers who have no direct knowledge of each employee's contributions calibrate the final rewards to ensure the final counts fit into the percentages laid out by the bell curve.

Adding Value-Based Motivators to a Performance-Management Program

Recalibrating rewards alongside company culture and employee engage-ment can drive higher productivity than rewards alone can. Employees value nonmonetary rewards as well as monetary compensation — especially in organizations that consolidate rewards at the top with a bell curve approach and with executive daily earnings that exceed what the average wages an employees earn in a week or more. These nonmonetary rewards include employees' day-to-day experience and their sense of purpose, connected-ness, and simple appreciation from their superiors and colleagues. Alto-gether, these rewards create loyalty and commitment.

Another model for value-based rewards could be found with the Navy Seals or other military special forces, who do not compete for monetary rewards but nevertheless have high-performing environments. Applicants to these jobs endure extreme conditions in order to be chosen among the select few who can wear the uniform and insignia of these elite units. Many other less dangerous jobs (such as those in the scientific community, health care, and teaching) also attract highly talented individuals for the honor of work-ing with the cream of the crop in their industry versus the promise of high compensation. Therefore, if companies manage their brand and become best of class in their industry, they may not need not rely on pay and com-pensation alone to attract top talent.

One last consideration when developing a reward and compensation model is that independent consultants work for a fixed, agreed-upon cost with an upward expectation of excellence from the client — without earning merit increases, bonuses, or stock options. Despite not having a pot of gold at the end of the rainbow, good contractors and consultants consistently perform at high levels and continue to hone their professional skills out of a sense of pride and to remain competitive in the market. The key here is that money is not the only solution to attracting and retaining top talent.

Although managers cannot always control internal policies, quotas, and the performance-management framework, managers can implement some value-based principles locally within their teams. Rather than hinging employee appreciation to the performance-management and compensation model, managers overcome the stigma around performance management by providing continuous feedback, career growth opportunities, mentoring, and other rewards, such as training or industry conferences. Further, managers can often influence the extent to which rewards and compensation for direct reports encourage competition or reward teamwork. With these points in mind, the following sections focus on management practices that can add value to a performance-management program.

Connecting with employees

Managers who don't engage employees cripple the value of any performance-management framework. For example, when managers don't hold one-on-one meetings, staff meetings, or strategy/planning meetings and no effective feedback mechanisms are in place, employees will not trust manager's feedback on their performance. In contrast, managers who engage direct reports frequently are more likely to provide an accurate assessment of performance. This approach creates a connectedness with direct reports, enabling the manager to access real-life knowledge of the employee's environment, behavior, and relative contributions when preparing performance reviews or attending calibration meetings. To create this sense of trust and connectedness, managers need to engage with employees on an ongoing basis, typically with the following regular meetings:

- Cyclic one-on-one meetings with individual employees
- Weekly staff and monthly strategic meetings to provide a forum to discuss issues and changes in priorities
- Periodic all-hands events (quarterly at a minimum) to share accomplishments, the status on scorecard objectives, and changes in priorities and to ensure information is being cascaded through the organization. Get feedback in a public forum.

- Direct engagement by walking around and talking to associates or picking up the phone and calling employees just to check in.

Good leaders may even attend skip-level meetings with employees at all levels to observe how associates interact and how their personal brand represents the department. Skip-level meetings may include technical design reviews, blueprint playback, and user acceptance testing.

Connecting with employees regularly establishes greater trust with employees when providing feedback on their accomplishments or areas for improvement.

With real-time knowledge of each contributor's outcomes, managers do not need to wait until mid- or end-of-year to reward employees for specific accomplishments or point out their areas for improvement. In this model, if the employee is still failing at the end-of-year and no coaching has occurred to solve this, it is the manager's failure, not the employee's.

Providing career growth and mentoring opportunities

Managers can often spend some discretionary money to help employees grow their careers. For example, sending employees to an industry conference is a good tool for growing organizational talent because employees expand their network with colleagues from similar companies who face the same challenges and work directly with industry experts.

For employees who have become stuck on a treadmill, complacent, or apathetic, these opportunities can renew employees' interest in their work. They remember what they loved about the industry, the work, and the innovations, and it can rekindle this fire internally when they return to their companies. Furthermore, these adventures sometimes renew the associate in ways that cannot be quantified.

If companies can spare a number of team members simultaneously, attending a conference can be a team-building experience, creating trust and better alignment.

Finally, an added bonus is each associate can be asked to come back and present their findings or make recommendations, giving them a chance to polish their presentation skills or champion a transformational project for the organization. These are all building blocks to helping employees build confidence, experience, and engagement, as well as providing critical IT consulting service in-house.

Clarifying how a performance-management program works

The easiest way for a manager to overcome the performance-management conundrum is complete honesty and transparency with team members about how the system works or does not work. Explain the challenges, show compassion and empathy, and then architect a mutually agreeable strategy that demonstrates a commitment to employees' success. Decouple the idea of compensation from high performance. Provide a culture where employees would gladly trade a few dollars for the opportunity to be a part of the team and something bigger than themselves.

Managers may also be able to use their limited authority to shape how the rewards and compensation is implemented for their direct reports. The following sections explain three fundamental shifts that managers may be able to make and communicate to their teams in order to change how the performance-management program is perceived.

Consultant model: Create a standard pricing mindset

To overcome obstacles to performance management, managers must first ensure employees' base salaries are competitive and fair for the value employees provide. This is accomplished by gathering industry data for key resources performing similar roles in similar companies and/or industries, including collecting quantitative data on compensation for contractors for comparison. This data can be used to level and adjust salaries across the workforce as well as create transparency for team members about the criteria being used in determining salary ranges for the company. The goal is to develop an independent contractor mindset with employees, so that they understand their compensation and benefits are already competitive, independent of a fraction of a percentage point on their merit increases and bonuses. Another goal is to ensure compensation is fair relative to each person's experience and contribution.

Remember, independent consultants are on a fixed-fee model. There are no merit increases each year, bonuses, or stock options that influence the outcomes. Performance is driven by one's personal desire to manage a reputation and provide high-quality value to the client at an agreed-upon price.

Reward-leveling model: Spread the wealth; do not concentrate it

Even when organizations use performance ratings to determine compensation, managers typically have some discretion in how to apply the compensation allotted to their teams. Instead of giving the highest share of rewards to a few, managers can use a leveling exercise to ensure the pool of money is more fairly distributed, independent of the rating system. In this approach, managers and employees recognize that a fraction of a percentage point does not really amount to a significant shift in dollars, thereby promoting a shared rewards system for the combined success of the team.

The goal of the leveling exercise is to take the focus off competing for the coveted winning slots predetermined by the organization's performance-management quotas (bell curve). Managers still operate within the margins provided, but architect a system of compensating employees consistently and fairly. Underperformers are dealt with throughout the year, not just at the end of the year. This approach takes into account each individual's ability to perform their job relative to base salary, not seniority. It is expected that team members have different levels of competence and therefore have different base salaries. It's not accurate to rank and rate employees at different salaries and tenure with the same expectation for contribution. Therefore, those who contribute more or who are more experienced should already make higher salaries versus higher salaries and bonuses.

Peer and business partner surveys: Create measurements employees trust

To measure employees based on their accomplishments or to pinpoint areas for improvement, managers need qualitative data. In addition to details gathered over the course of the year or evaluation period through employee engagement, managers can also use peer and business partner surveys as a tool used consistently across a group of people performing similar roles to measure outcomes over which those people have control.

With peer and business partner surveys, here are the keys to success:

- Employees agree to the criteria.
- Employees understand the relationship of their contribution to the scorecard and IT goals.
- Employees trust the process to collect feedback.

In a typical a peer and business partner survey, peers are fellow team members and the business partner may be a customer, stakeholder, or another technical service center that the team supports. The peer and business partner surveys serve as a standard and repeatable process to gather data, which can be used to do the following:

- Measure adoption of the company's culture and behaviors.

- Recognize achievements or pinpoint areas for improvement.
- Develop qualitative reports that both employees and managers can trust.

Although an organization can share a common tool, framework, workflow, and approach, the survey criteria is developed at the team or technical service center level. To ensure employees trust the measurements, teams collaborate on determining the success factors and language. Managers align criteria with the scorecard for the team and performance management criteria. Performance reviews are also updated to track the same criteria. After the key measurements are defined, the survey is finalized, and the survey cycle is published and shared with all participants, as shown in Figure 11-2.

Figure 11-2

The survey process can be manual (using email, a Word document, or Excel workbook) or can use any number of internal or external tools, keeping in mind the time and effort required for compiling and building survey results. Managers keep survey information confidential to maintain trust and share scores only in aggregate with each associate.

The following list is an example of a peer and business partner survey focused on six key competencies:

- **Delivers on commitments:** How well does the employee meet their agreed-upon deadlines and commitments? Do they do what they said they would do?

- **Delivers high-quality work:** Demonstrates personal commitment and drive to set and then meet or exceed high standards and objectives while displaying a stretch-goal mentality.

- **Focuses on the customer:** Ensures that the customer perspective is a driving force behind business decisions and activities, thereby implementing service practices and solutions that anticipate and meet customers' needs.

- **Influences others:** Promotes ideas and proposals persuasively, shaping people's opinions. Wins buy-in for initiatives and works through conflicts while building positive working relationships.

- **Collaborates well with team members and customers:** Develops and uses collaborative relationships to facilitate the accomplishment of work and business goals. Listens well and demonstrates sensitivity to others' opinions and feelings.

- **Is decisive and shows sound judgment:** Selects clear and sometimes bold choices from among complex alternatives in a timely but fact-based manner. Consistently demonstrates sound judgment, making successful decisions even in risky and ambiguous situations.

- **Comments:** The survey may include an opportunity to provide free-form feedback about accomplishments or areas for improvement.

Each question requires the ability to grade on a scale. Ideally, survey responders can easily understand each scale setting. Further, where possible, scales should be aligned with performance-management criteria, because employees are already accustomed to the company's grading process. Table 11-1 is an example of rating choices that include some brief text to describe criteria for each choice.

Table 11-1 Sample Survey Scale

Rating	What It Indicates	Corresponding Performance Management Criteria
5	Far exceeds expectations	Outperformed most others. Consistently exceeded expectations.
4	Exceeds expectations	Outperformed many others. Frequently exceeded expectations.
3	Meets expectations	Solid performer who occasionally exceeded expectations.
2	Below expectations	Inconsistent performance. Did not meet expectations in some key areas.
1	Does not meet expectations	Unacceptable performance. Immediate improvement required.
N		Not observed or learning curve, such as new in role

The ideal survey creates a systematic way to gather intelligence for evaluating performance while keeping the process and overhead low. Results should remain confidential and reflect only each individual's contribution, rather than rank all employees based on survey results, because the data is not absolute. One team member could be on a long-term project with a disgruntled business unit. Peers or customers could provide extremely high marks that are undeserved. Survey responders can be fickle and even their mood on a given day may shift a rating one point either way.

Although peer and business partner surveys can provide insights into the experience of peers and customers, these surveys cannot be the sole determining factor in performance management or used to rank against one team member against another.

An employee self-assessment can also provide insight and pinpoint any disconnect between the employee's self-perception and how others perceive them, as shown in Figure 11-3. Often, employees do not know where the blind spot is until this type of review is performed.

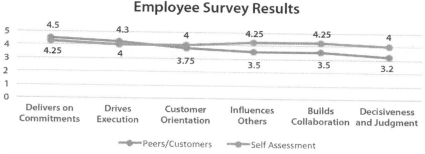

Figure 11-3

Understanding the distance between the employee's perceived performance and the colleagues' or customers' actual experience becomes a tool to open a dialog for a mentoring or learning moment. A manager might ask the associate what factors might be influencing their personal brand when scores are significantly lower than expected.

Chapter Summary

It's time to question the collective wisdom of company cultures still working from outdated performance-management models and compensation practices, such as the bell curve, to drive higher productivity. Companies should consider a new approach to performance management with a guiding principle to drive success for all employees, not just the top 30 percent. Unfortunately, when only the highest performers receive the highest share of rewards, the performance-management program drives behaviors counterproductive to providing the value proposition for clients of IT.

In fact, better employee engagement and organizational health will provide a sustainable increase in productivity over bonuses and rewards. By reducing the focus on annual rewards, companies find new ways to retain talented employees through culture and competitive base pay.

Remember, performance management is not just once or twice year. Managers need to provide continuous feedback for the associate, taking time to send a congratulations or a small gift of appreciation for a job well done, as well as to point out areas for improvement without a formal performance document. Managers should provide this feedback on an ongoing basis during staff meeting observations, one-on-one meetings, skip-level drop-in meetings, and through the employee's outcomes or status reports. There should be no surprises at review time.

Additionally, a peer and business partner survey can be valuable if the employees are involved in designing it, trust the measurements, and have clarity about what they are being measured on. However, surveys and metrics make up only part of an associate's overall evaluation. Managers must remain connected with their direct reports and their ongoing contributions.

Managers should reduce the importance of the rating system itself by opening an honest dialog with associates regarding the limitations of the performance-management process. In other words, admit the system does not work as expected at times. Remove the fear of losing rewards by setting an expectation that there is no guarantee of a high rating. When employees are no longer afraid of the grade they will receive, they feel less defensive about feedback from a performance review, which enables a more meaningful discussion on those things that are important:

- Reviewing progress against defined objectives
- Reviewing feedback from peer and business partner surveys
- Developing a coaching strategy for setbacks
- Recognizing major and minor accomplishments
- Discussing top strengths for the year
- Calling out areas for improvement for the next year

Finally, because compensation is based on a budget pool, employees need transparency to understand how merit increases, bonuses, and/or restricted stock units are determined for a group or individually. There should be full disclosure with employees about how compensation is calculated and what the available pool is each year.

But all these strategies can take a company only so far. In the end, organizations need to be careful not to be a pennywise and pound foolish. A fraction of a percent for larger merit increase or bonus often equates to a few thousand dollars for an employee and perhaps even $25,000 for an entire team whose OPEX budget is in the millions. That's a small price to pay for a group of people who sacrificed their evenings, weekends, and sometimes vacations for the company's success. Remember rewards for employee's performance should not tied to the company's future but look back to where they have been and what the employees have done.

CHAPTER 12

LEADERSHIP

"Not finance. Not strategy. Not technology. It is teamwork that remains the ultimate competitive advantage, both because it is so powerful and so rare."
— Patrick Lencioni, *The Five Dysfunctions of a Team*

Throughout this book, I refer to IT leadership, business leadership, and team managers because these roles are critical to the success of any IT project or transformation as well as the day-to-day operations. Stepping back to consider what makes an effective leader can help anyone in these roles shepherd the IT organization and the people within it to success, and this chapter provides a framework to reflect on your leadership style as well as discover resources to explore this topic further.

Prioritizing Your Time

During a recent teleseminar, "A Chat with Merideth Mehlberg, Executive Coach and Career Strategist, on 'From Doer to Leader: Redefining how you win on the job,'" Mehlberg described leadership using a simple and compelling framework: "Great leaders stop trying to be the superstars and rather create superstars and super cultures. They no longer focus on the details, projects, or tasks for day-to-day operations. Good leaders do less and accomplish more by prioritizing their time on the right activities."

Mehlberg advocates thinking of your focus in terms of a pie chart of how time is spent, as shown in Figure 12-1, and warns that spending more than 15 percent of your time on operations can create a culture of control, where people are cautious. In essence, when leaders don't give employees autonomy over their work, employees come to believe that leaders don't trust them to do their jobs and become dependent on leaders to make decisions.

Ideal Leadership Focus

Figure 12-1

> If leaders find themselves chained to their desks performing operational duties, unable to spend 35 percent of the time developing personal connections with their team members and stakeholders, it's possible they are micromanaging their teams.

Empowering people

When leaders are managing their time effectively, they can invest time in enabling their people to move fully into roles while not keeping constant tabs on them out of a need for control or fear. The following practices can help leaders effectively manage and empower their teams and employees:

- Give teams the opportunity and autonomy to take on harder assignments. Leaders need to resist the urge to do it themselves.

- Leaders who provide all the answers disempower team members. Therefore, good leaders make it safe for everyone to innovate by building confidence in team members first and being patient that the competency will follow.

- When mistakes happen, leaders treat areas for improvement as coaching or learning moments.

- Establish personal connections and create a sense of community across the team. To do this, leaders must understand themselves first and then contextualize their style with an awareness of what motivates each team member.

Ultimately, leaders are responsible for building the scaffolding, providing mentoring, and creating the environment to get team members involved and committed. Leaders set the tone for the organization and for the teams that are expected to deliver on the IT promise. When teams are effectively managed, share trust and core values, and have clarity about expected outcomes, then commitment and successful outcomes increase. In contrast, leaders' using fear, intimidation, or coercion to motivate employees is symptomatic of a problem either with the leader or with the organizational culture.

When goals and objectives are clear, the philosophy is locally owned and relevant to the team, employees understand what high performance looks like, and a correction in course should just feel like mentoring. If the measurements for performance is fair, trusted, and understood by all, there can be little debate about whether employees are meeting or failing to meet expectations. Remember, the Navy Seals and NYFD do not to incentivize team members to perform with bonuses, rewards, or stock options to ensure outstanding performance. Instead, they foster and draw upon a common purpose, tribal culture, and code of conduct everyone lives by, including leadership.

Focusing on strategy

What does spending 50 percent of one's time on strategy mean? The Six Protocols provide the framework for developing and focusing the IT strategy. Leaders always have opportunities to drive improvements in the following six areas:

- Defining and refining the IT business model (Understanding customers, the IT value proposition, and key partnerships; managing assets, cost structures, and so on)
- Developing and updating the IT roadmap for technology and governance to support the business and the IT ecosystem
- Providing and optimizing the infrastructure (Processes, staffing, and skills) and developing measurements to track progress (IT scorecards)
- Architecting and continuously improving the strategic-sourcing approach to provide better controls and improve vendor outcomes
- Managing the customer's experience by managing the IT brand
- Maintaining organizational health (Addressing employee engagement, performance management, and compensation and also modeling leadership)

The IT strategy facilitates teamwork. The strategy is what gets everyone in the boat, rowing in the same direction.

Building Your Brand as a Leader

Whether you're new to a leadership role or have been managing others for years, reflecting on your personal brand as a leader can give you new energy and insight for leading and empowering your teams. The following sections highlight the importance of modeling desired behaviors and provide tips and thoughts to help those who are new to leadership roles successfully make the transition.

Modeling positive behaviors

Leaders who effectively manage people inspire them and create a shared enthusiasm about the work they do. They model the right behaviors, including humility by admitting mistakes. They build trust, ensure accountability, and encourage healthy debate across teams in order to find the best solutions in the shortest amount of time. Leadership is being mindful, objective, understanding, and gaining the respect of your employees, peers, business partners, and customers through actions rather than words.

The commitment to leadership has to be more than posters, slogans, or something managers talk about in quarterly all-hands meetings or offsite events. It's the brand everyone creates every day in interactions such as the following:

- **Emails**: As I discuss in Chapter 9, effective emails are organized, have a professional tone, and clearly ask for what is needed and when it is needed. Further, employees read emails from senior leaders first and more carefully. Every email sent can influence the employee's assessment of a leader's connection with the IT organization —or lack thereof if the email is inaccurate.

- **Phone calls:** Pick up the phone and call people. Teach your associates to do the same. Mentor them not to rely on email or instant messaging. Encourage employees to periodically consider a human connection with their peers or customers. Often, a phone call can save everyone time.

- **Meetings:** Meetings are the most important tool for setting the standards or code of conduct for behavior. All eyes are on the leaders in every meeting. Are leaders organized, focused, and actively listening to the input of others? Can they manage through difficult issues, handle healthy conflict, and foster collaboration where it may not exist?

- **Hallway or elevator discussions:** Leaders should avoid criticizing, condemning or complaining (the 3 Cs) when in public places. They also should be slow to listen to slander and discourage this when it occurs around them.

- **Choices or decisions:** Leaders should have high standards, even under extreme emotional discomfort. After coming to a decision, leaders trust their decision-making process and let their outcomes be their truth.

Shifting into a leadership role

As leaders move through progressive levels of management, they need to be mindful of their own transformation and journey as they shift from doer to the next stage of leader, because people often feel a sense of loss during that transition.

The familiar, easy, and instant gratification of completing a task, assignment, or project and receiving a reward (in emotional strokes) isn't the way you "win" as a leader. Rather, the spotlight is now on the achievements of the teams the leader manages.

With less recognition for one's own accomplishments, gratification comes from helping others grow and succeed. This change can involve a difficult personal transformation for many, and requires working without expectation of individual reward or recognition.

Leaders need to demonstrate confidence in themselves and their teams. As a leader, one cannot look for external confirmation on every decision and often must source their certainty from within. Good leaders eliminate self-importance, listen more, and contemplate other's beliefs before defending a position. They are self-aware and capable of aligning their style with the style of the people with whom they interact. Most importantly, they do not make decisions based on fear. Good leaders are willing to do things that are not popular, such as championing technology changes when dollars are sparse, requesting a budget increase to support growth, or requesting additional staffing when needed.

Exploring Resources on Leadership

You can find a number of great books on leadership. The following books have a place on any high-performing leader's professional bookshelf:

- *Leadership on the Line: Staying Alive through the Dangers of Leading* by Martin Linsky and Ronald A. Heifetz
- *Tribal Leadership: Leveraging Natural Groups to Build a Thriving Organization* by Dave Logan and John King
- *Teams at the Top* by Jon R. Katzenbach
- *The Wisdom of Teams* by Jon R. Katzenbach and Douglas K. Smith

Beyond the business book genre of the 20th and 21st centuries, I believe the ideals of good leadership can be also found in writings dating back 4th century B.C in some simple passages from the sage Lao-Tzu in the *Tao Teh King* (translation by Archie J. Bahm):

- Most intelligent leaders bring about results without making those controlled realize that they are being influenced.
- The less intelligent seek to motivate others by appeals to loyalty, honor, self-interest, and flattery.
- The worst try to force others to improve by condemning their conduct.
- Intelligent control appears as un-control or freedom.

Chapter Summary

Leadership is an essential factor in any IT transformation or project. Any new or experienced leader can benefit from stepping back to evaluate how they spend their time and take stock of their leadership style:

- How are you spending your time? Ideally, aim to spend 50 percent of your time on strategy, 35 percent on empowering employees, and 15 percent on operations. If you are having to solve all the operational problems, then something needs to change on the team.
- To empower your teams, give them autonomy while providing the scaffolding and opportunities to help them grow. Great leaders maintain ongoing communication with their teams and individual team members.
- Develop an IT strategy that looks holistically at all the factors that can influence the success or failure of the IT organization.
- To build your personal brand as a leader, give yourself time to take stock of what behaviors you model for your teams in your day-to-day behaviors and interactions.
- To continue to grow as a leader, explore books and other resources on leadership.

Employees recognize and are drawn to good leaders.
What motivates employees is not fear but honesty,
confidence, loyalty, integrity, and fairness.

CONNECTING THE DOTS

If you have made it this far, you will probably indulge me for a few more paragraphs so I can explain why I wrote this book. IT is trending in the wrong direction, and after the last decade of a steady decline, I found myself at a career and life crossroads described by Douglas LaBier, surviving at great emotional cost due to conditions that were good for the advancement of the career but not the spirit.

So I decided quit to my job at a Fortune 15 company, cash in my stock, pay off my house, and take the summer off before trying something new. After retreating to the desert to reflect on my career choices (actually the Hyatt Spa and Resort in Scottsdale, AZ), I decided to write a blueprint of how I would approach building a sustainable IT organization. I truly believe with the right strategy, focus, and communication, IT organizations can successfully adapt to any business challenge, deliver on commitments, and build a culture where employees thrive.

There Is No Turnkey Solution

My first objective was to encourage companies to stop buying into the "cheaper, faster, better" gimmicks or using profit-based motives to drive IT decision making. These are not the right approaches because IT is not simply a financial problem to solve.

Further, companies need to ignore what industry experts are promoting this month or year, because the mounting evidence shows that no single script, template, or standard practice is plug-and-play for every organization, department, or technical service center. In contrast, companies need to roll up their sleeves and do the hard work (which I've outlined in the Six Protocols), rather than handing over the organization's destiny to outside consulting or outsourcing firms. Remember, what motivates these vendors may not be in the company's best interest. There is an old saying in the consulting circles: "If you're not part of the solution, there's good money to me made prolonging the problem."

I believe that, in order to remain competitive when managing IT projects and operations, IT organizations need to follow a value-based approach that is flexible and adaptive because IT processes and strategies change rapidly, just like the technology and applications they support.

By doing so successful IT organizations take into consideration all Six Protocols in concert. If properly designed, the IT strategy, delivery methodology, and strategic-sourcing approaches blend into the organization so they are indistinguishable to the business, IT shared services, managed services, and the dedicated IT workforce. *The Six Protocols of IT Transformation* provides a framework and common language for how IT organizations can reliably deliver outstanding benefits to both internal and external customers.

> The real value of IT is not measured by the cost savings realized. Rather, it is measured by the benefits provided to customers and by improving the client's condition.

Finding a Solution with the Six Protocols

The statistics around failed projects, outsourcing, and employee satisfaction leave little room for argument that the current trajectory of IT is trending in the wrong direction. Further, a profit-based approach (such as "cheaper, faster, better") only exacerbates the problems facing IT. This book has taken the reader on a journey of how real IT transformation can happen. Remember, IT transformation is a four-stage approach that encompasses six discrete but interlocking protocols.

Here's how the Six Protocols integrate with each stage:

1. Assess the current belief systems in IT that influence decision-making around the IT strategy and drive the wrong behaviors.

2. Understand when industry trends are contributing to challenges and problems faced by IT (by seeing the world through the eyes of the IT workforce).

3. Build a roadmap (First through Fifth Protocols) with the IT value proposition in mind to clarify what employees' strategic focus is and to increase IT success.

4. Align the workforce and customers behind a set of common goals and foster a healthy culture (the Sixth Protocol, organizational health).

As IT organizations progress through these four stages and the Six Protocols, IT leadership and management needs to keep in mind the most important question to be answered with any approach: Does the proposed strategy improve the client's condition or reduce the ability of IT to serve its customers and deliver on the agreed IT value proposition?

Final Thoughts on Managing IT Transformation

What I am suggesting in this book is a change in the way IT is managed: Shift more decision-making authority to the middle-level managers and local IT teams. When decision-making is centralized with senior management, who may not have all the information, the decision-makers are often too far removed from the day-to-day impacts of those decisions.

In the *value-based* model, leadership is no longer a top-down approach, and middle managers as well as individual contributors play a larger role in architecting and driving needed changes in the organization. By being more inclusive, employees feel more connected to strategy, understand what's expected, and take more accountability for the outcomes.

IT leadership can no longer think of employees simply as homogenized commodities that are replaceable, bought and sold at the lowest price to achieve financial targets. Instead, companies must consider applying value-based principles to their strategy around people, processes, and technology. Remember, when everyone has access to the same technologies, methodologies, and vendors, the ultimate competitive advantage remains with the people.

Man really attains the state of complete humanity when he produces, without being forced by physical need to sell himself as a commodity. — *Che Guevara*

BIBLIOGRAPHY
AND REFERENCE

Godin, Seth. *Linchpin*. Penguin Group, 2010.

Joiner, Brain L. *Fourth Generation Management*. McGraw-Hill Professional, 2014.

LaBier, Douglas. *Modern Madness: The Hidden Link between Work and Emotional Conflict*. Addison-Wesley, 1986.

Lao-Tzu, *Tao Teh King*. Translated by Archie J. Bahm. World Books, 1986.

Logan, Dave, John King, and Halee Fischer-Write. *Tribal Leadership*. Harper Business, 2011.

Phillips, Stephen Scott. *Control Your ERP Destiny*. Stephen Scott Phillips, 2013.

Pink, Daniel H. *Drive*. New York: Riverhead Books, New York: Penguin Group, 1995.

Online References

Bloch, Michael, Sven Blumberg, and Jürgen Laartz. "Delivering Large-Scale IT Projects On Time, On Budget, and On Value." Study by the University of Oxford, October 2012. McKinsey & Company. http://www.mckinsey.com/insights/business_technology/delivering_large-scale_it_projects_on_time_on_budget_and_on_value

Calleam Consulting Ltd. "Why Do Projects Fail?" 2015. http://calleam.com/WTPF/?page_id=1445

"Gartner Paper, Gartner Says Smart Organizations Will Embrace Fast and Frequent Project Failure in Their Quest for Agility." 2013. http://www.gartner.com/newsroom/id/2477816

"Gartner's Ed Holub on ITIL." 2006. http://www.baselinemag.com/c/a/IT-Management/QA-Gartners-Ed-Holub-on-ITIL#

"Geneca Study, Doomed from the Start, Why 75% Business and Executives Anticipate Their Software Development Projects Will Fail." 2011. http://www.geneca.com/75-business-executives-anticipate-software-projects-fail/

IBM Corporation. "Making Change Work." 2008. http://www-935.ibm.com/services/us/gbs/bus/pdf/gbe03100-usen-03-making-change-work.pdf

KPMG. "Global IT Project Management Survey." 2005. http://www.kpmg.com.au/Portals/0/irmpmqa-global-it-pm-survey2005.pdf

"Panorama, Scope Overruns and Suboptimal Benefit Realization Continue to Plague ERP Implementations." 2014. http://panorama-consulting.com/resource-center/2014-erp-report/

Reed, Brad. "Apple Employee Quits His Job, Spill Dirt on 'What Really Goes On' There." BGR, April 2015. http://bgr.com/2015/04/08/what-is-working-at-apple-really-like/

Statistic Brain Research Institute. "Job Outsourcing Statistics." 2014. http://www.statisticbrain.com/outsourcing-statistics-by-country/

Toufexis, A. "Living Struggling for Sanity." Time, October 8, 1990. http://www.time.com/time/magazine

33878487R00123

Made in the USA
San Bernardino, CA
14 May 2016